**Our Kitchen.
Our Mission.
Your Experience.**

*Remember, you can't
lick the bowl watching
The Food Channel!*

This book is dedicated:

To my Ami-Grammers for my earliest memories of cooking – sitting on the kitchen counter to help her make pie dough – I'll always be your "Laurie Annie Oakley."

To my amazing boys, Delaney and Devin, for sitting on MY counter when they were little to help me cook and for making the time in their busy lives to let me cook for them.

To my sister, Lynne, for providing the technical and emotional support, along with comic relief, so that I could finally get this important project to print.

To my Mom for making sure we sat around the table for dinner, for making sure we had a birthday celebration no matter what, and for inspiring me to cook with her own passion for creating delicious food.

To my neighbors, Tony & Maria Pagano, for always asking me to come in and eat dinner with them every time I knocked on their neighboring door and for exposing me to authentic Italian culture throughout my childhood.

To all the home cooks who do their best to put good food on the table, regardless of their skill level or resources.

To the friends and family who have gathered around tables with me over the years to help create a beautiful patchwork of life memories because to me, all of the important things in life happen around the table.

Best Recipes
Second Collection

Laura Laiben
"The Main Dish"

Copyright © 2013 by
The Culinary Center of Kansas City, L.C.
Overland Park, Kansas 66204

Publisher: The Culinary Center of Kansas City, L.C.
Recipe Selection: Laura Laiben
Graphic Artist: Joel Herman (Urban Art)
Production: Lynne Parker & Laura Laiben
Printed in Korea by asianprinting.com

ISBN: 978-0-9859691-0-3

Additional copies of The Culinary Center of Kansas City – Best Recipes – Second Collection may be purchased:
- *via email: cook@kcculinary.com*
- *online at: www.kcculinary.com*
- *via phone: 913-341-4455*
- *via USPS: The Culinary Center of Kansas City, 7920 Santa Fe, Overland Park, KS 66204*

Table Of Contents

Introduction   *2*

Lesson One: **Small Plates & Starters**   *5*

Lesson Two: **Salads & Dressings**   *21*

Lesson Three: **Soups**   *33*

Lesson Four: **Main Dishes**   *45*

Lesson Five: **Pasta**   *63*

Lesson Six: **Vegetarian & Side Dishes**   *79*

Lesson Seven: **Breads**   *91*

Lesson Eight: **Desserts**   *99*

Lesson Nine: **Little Extras**   *117*

Recipe Index   *127*

About The Author   *128*

Introduction

Each day I get to turn the key in the door of my dream. I realize that not many people get to say that. My dream was to create a venue in the Midwest where culinarians of all skill levels could come together in a relaxed and non-intimidating environment to celebrate the culinary arts in a wide variety of ways and to explore the ever-increasing role that food and wine plays in our lives and around our tables. Since 1998 I have been consistently living that dream in a very real way.

Housed in a beautifully restored 6500 square foot turn-of-the-century buggy barn in the Kansas City suburb of Overland Park, Kansas, are two spacious teaching kitchens, a large event space, offices, and a retail store. In this amazing space (and off-site as well), we offer over 600 contemporary classes and demonstrations in the culinary arts each year and hundreds of interactive cooking parties, culinary events and teambuilding experiences. In addition we are home to the Midwest BBQ Institute™, Junior Chefs Academy™, "All Hands For Hunger™" interactive cooking parties with a community service purpose, CookWell!™ corporate wellness program, Dinners on Demand™ frozen chef-prepared dishes for sale to the public, a monthly "Staff Lunch" open to the public as well as a thriving retail shop called "Kitchenology.™" Who would have guessed? I certainly didn't.

Our cooking class instructors range from professional chefs to grass roots cooks eager to share their culinary expertise and provide a high quality educational experience to our students and customers. Our classes and events are designed to dispel the myth that cooking is difficult and mysterious and to recognize the importance of each individual cook and their abilities. I believe that it is not secret recipes or an arsenal of fancy tools that make a good cook but rather the application of fundamental cooking techniques, the selection of quality ingredients, the proper handling of food and equipment and the willingness to experiment. And oh yes, a cook must always have a sense of humor!

My inspiration for The Culinary Center was the incredible women and men I watched and learned from as I grew up in a small town in Missouri whose silent mission it was to continue their own culinary heritage and traditions in their everyday lives. My most vivid and nurturing childhood memories are those found in the kitchen and backyard of my Grandmother's house where pie crusts were rolled, green beans snapped, corn shucked and dumplings formed all to the music of laughter and love. My Mom was an experimental cook and truly understood the importance of creating memorable events around food as well. I also spent a lot of time in the home and restaurant kitchen of my Italian neighbors where I was exposed to authentic European cuisine. It wasn't until years later did I realize how much I instinctively knew about cooking.

One of my goals, even before we opened our doors in May of 1998, was to produce a cookbook which actually happened in 2000 with the "The Best Recipes of The Culinary Center of Kansas City – First Collection." It has been 13 years since then and high time for an encore. This second collection contains some of my all-time favorite recipes garnered from our classes, caterings, special events, culinary travels, guest instructors and from my own personal collection. I have also included a few of the recipes from the First Collection that I believed worthy of reprint. There were literally hundreds of recipes that did not make it into these pages. It certainly wasn't because they weren't worthy – only that there wasn't enough room.

Many have described The Culinary Center as warm, inviting, transporting and sacred. It certainly is sacred ground to me. I am so proud each time I turn that key to open the door. The Culinary Center holds my dreams in physical form and represents something that I have built with my own heart. I cannot tell you the joy I feel that the community has embraced this novel concept. It continues to exceed my wildest expectations. Having practiced law for many years prior to jumping career tracks to pursue my passion, I truly believe that The Culinary Center is an example of what happens when you take the courageous (Yes, I will call myself courageous!) leap off the edge into the unknown and wings magically appear.

Laura Laiben
"The Main Dish"

Lesson One

Small Plates & Starters

Artichoke, Asiago, and Spinach Dip

Blue Cheese, Bacon and Onion Savory Cheesecake

Brie en Croute with Apricot Chutney

Crab Diablo Stuffed Mushrooms

Curried Mango Shrimp

Devilishly Good Deviled Eggs

Gougeres (French Cheese Puffs)

'Inside Out' Crab Rangoon Dip with Wonton Chips

Sweet Potato Empanadas with
Beef Picadillo Filling and Harissa Sauce

Moroccan Market Spicy Roasted Nuts

"Secret Ingredient" Spinach Dip

Truffled Lentil Spoons with Bacon Vinaigrette

White Bean and Swiss Chard Bruschetta

Artichoke, Asiago, and Spinach Dip

A great version of a timeless appetizer. When our chefs make this dip for our guests, we secretly hope they will make extra for the staff! We love it as a spread on crostini or crackers, but we've also been known to eat it by the spoonful. It's that good!

2 tablespoons olive oil
1 large onion, peeled, diced
¼ cup garlic, fresh, minced
3 cups spinach, fresh, washed, dried
1 pound cream cheese
2 cups sour cream
3 cups artichoke hearts, canned, drained, chopped
¼ cup lemon juice, freshly squeezed
½ pound Asiago cheese, shredded
1 tablespoon whole grain mustard
3 tablespoons hot pepper sauce
Salt and freshly ground pepper to taste

Preheat oven to 350 degrees. In a skillet heat oil and sauté onion and garlic for 2 to 3 minutes or until softened, stirring constantly to prevent burning. Transfer to a large mixing bowl. Add spinach, cream cheese, sour cream, artichokes, juice, Asiago cheese, mustard, pepper sauce, salt, and pepper. Using a large spoon, stir until ingredients are combined. Transfer mixture to a baking dish and cover with a sheet of aluminum foil. Place in oven and bake for 15 minutes or until mixture is bubbly. Remove from oven and uncover. Serve warm. Makes about 6 to 8 cups.

Blue Cheese, Bacon and Onion Savory Cheesecake

A CCKC favorite for many years! Guess you can't beat a great recipe. It is rich, sinful and the perfect hearty appetizer. Oh, and it freezes well too. You can't go wrong with this one!

CRUST
1 cup bread crumbs
½ cup parmesan cheese, grated
2 tablespoons butter, unsalted, melted

FILLING
2 pounds cream cheese, room temperature
4 large eggs
½ cup cream
½ cup bacon, cooked, crumbled
2 tablespoons butter, unsalted, melted
1 onion, diced
½ pound blue cheese, crumbled
½ teaspoon salt
½ teaspoon black pepper
3 to 4 drops hot pepper sauce

¼ cup scallions, finely chopped, for garnish

Preheat oven to 260 degrees. For the crust, line a 10" spring form pan with aluminum foil. In a mixing bowl add bread crumbs, cheese, and butter and stir to combine. Transfer to pan. Using hands (or back of spoon) press crust into the bottom of pan. Set aside.

For the filling, in a large mixing bowl add cream cheese, eggs, and cream and mix thoroughly. Add bacon, butter, onion, blue cheese, salt, pepper, and hot sauce and stir to incorporate all ingredients well. Using a spatula, transfer cheese mixture to prepared springform pan, scraping sides to remove all of the mixture and smooth to cover entire pan. Place in oven and bake for 90 minutes or until puffed and golden. Turn oven off and allow cheesecake to sit in oven an additional 30 minutes. Remove from oven and place in refrigerator overnight or until thoroughly chilled and set. (Cheesecake can be made up to 3 days ahead of time.)

To serve, remove cheesecake from refrigerator.
Top with scallions, for garnish. Serve with crackers.
Makes 20 to 40 appetizer servings.

Etc.

Serve with salted rice crackers which are usually packaged in tubes and can be found in the deli section of most grocery stores. The combination of the salted crispiness of the cracker with the smooth and tangy texture of the cheesecake is perfect!

Brie en Croute with Apricot Chutney

A simple and impressive appetizer. The chutney makes a great hostess gift all on its own too.

Etc.

Don't be afraid to use a prepared chutney if you are in a pinch.

CHUTNEY
12 ounces dried apricots, chopped
1 large red onion, peeled, diced
1 cup water
2/3 cup cider vinegar
2/3 cup golden brown sugar, packed
3/4 cup tart cherries, dried
3 cloves garlic, fresh, peeled, finely chopped
2 teaspoons lemon peel, freshly zested
1/2 teaspoon kosher salt
1/8 teaspoon cayenne pepper

CHEESE
1 (8-inch) wheel brie cheese
1 (12-inch) sheet puff pastry
1 large egg, lightly beaten

For the chutney, in a heavy medium saucepan add apricots, onion, water, vinegar, brown sugar, cherries, garlic, lemon zest, salt, and cayenne pepper. Bring to a boil over medium-high heat and cook until all sugar is dissolved, stirring constantly. Reduce heat to medium low and continue to simmer for 20 minutes or until all liquid is absorbed and chutney is thick, stirring occasionally. Remove from heat and set aside.

For the cheese, preheat oven to 400 degrees. Unwrap cheese and place on a half-sheet baking sheet lined with parchment paper. Top with the pastry sheet. Gently stretch pastry over the edges of cheese to cover all sides. (You can decorate the top of pastry with scraps cut from the pastry, if desired.) With a pastry brush, lightly coat the top of pastry with egg. Place in oven and bake for 15 minutes or until deep golden brown. (If cheese leaks from pastry during baking, press pieces of foil over tear in pastry and continue baking.) Remove from oven. With a metal spatula, gently transfer cheese to a large serving platter. Arrange chutney around the cheese. Serve warm with French baguette slices, crostini or lavosh crackers. Makes approximately 12 appetizer servings.

Crab Diablo
Stuffed Mushrooms

An appetizers reception staple here at
The Culinary Center. Can't go wrong with these.

2 (8-ounce) packages cream cheese, room temperature
2 green onions, washed, peeled, chopped
½ pound imitation crabmeat
1 tablespoon crushed red pepper flakes
1 tablespoon hot sauce
1 tablespoon lemon juice, freshly squeezed
Dash of garlic powder
Salt and freshly ground black pepper to taste
2 pounds button mushrooms, fresh, scrubbed,
*   stems removed*
2 cups bread crumbs
Spray canola oil

In a medium bowl add cream cheese, onions, crab,
red pepper, hot sauce, juice, garlic, salt, and pepper.
Stir until well combined. Cover bowl with a sheet of plastic
wrap and place in the refrigerator for 1 hour or until ready
to use.

To assemble, spoon cheese mixture into the mushroom caps,
evenly dividing. Place mushrooms on a large rimmed baking
sheet. Spoon bread crumbs on top of each cap, evenly
dividing, pressing down to pack. Lightly spray with oil.
Place in oven and bake for 12 to 15 minutes. Remove from
oven and transfer to a serving platter. Serve warm. Makes
approximately 24 appetizer servings.

Etc.

Feel free to substitute
the imitation crabmeat
with fresh, if your
budget allows. It will
add a lighter and more
authentic taste to the
dish.

Curried Mango Shrimp

I found a recipe in a magazine about 15 years ago and tried it. Over the next few months I tweaked the recipe and made what I think is one of our favorite appetizers. Even if you don't like curry, you'll love this dish!

½ cup prepared mango chutney (or peach chutney)
¾ cup cilantro, fresh, washed, finely chopped
¾ cup basil, fresh, washed, finely chopped
1 cup yogurt, plain, low-fat
3 pounds large shrimp, fresh, shelled, deveined
¼ cup extra virgin olive oil
3 tablespoons curry powder
1 heaping tablespoon salt
Freshly ground black pepper, to taste

12 lime wedges, for garnish

For the chutney, in a medium bowl add chutney, cilantro, basil, and yogurt. Gently stir to combine. Set aside.

Preheat a large skillet. In a large bowl add shrimp, oil, curry, salt, and pepper. Stir to coat well. Transfer to the skillet and sauté for 1 to 2 minutes or until shrimp are pink and curled. Remove from heat and transfer shrimp mixture to the herbed yogurt-chutney bowl. Using a large spoon, gently stir to combine. Transfer equal portions to individual small plates. Serve with lime wedges on the side, for garnish.
Makes 12 servings.

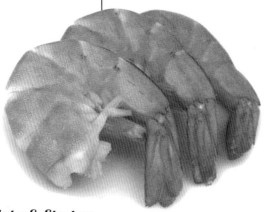

Devilishly Good
Deviled Eggs

Eggs and truffle oil. A perfect match. Done.

7 large eggs, hard boiled, peeled,
*   sliced in half lengthwise, divided*
¼ cup mayonnaise
1-½ tablespoons sweet pickle relish
½ teaspoon white truffle oil
2 tablespoons whole grain mustard
Salt and freshly ground black pepper to taste

Paprika, for garnish
Pimentos, for garnish

Remove yolks from the egg halves, reserving the whites, and transfer to a small bowl. Using a fork, mash the yolks. Add mayonnaise, relish, oil, mustard, salt, and pepper. Stir to combine well. Transfer the egg yolk mixture to a pastry bag fitted with a large star tip. Pipe the egg filling into the egg white halves, dividing evenly. Sprinkle paprika and pimentos over the tops, for garnish. Cover with a sheet of plastic wrap and place in the refrigerator until ready to serve. Serve cold. Makes 14 servings.

Etc.

Truffle oil has become a popular ingredient in the recipes of some of the most famous chefs but can be too expensive for the average home chef. Because of this growing popularity, a less expensive version of truffle oil is now showing up on store shelves in local grocery stores and specialty markets.

Gougeres
(French Cheese Puffs)

In Burgundy, where they originated, gougéres are considered the perfect hors d' oeuvre – complementary to wine and satisfying to the palate without being filling.

8 tablespoons butter, unsalted, cut into pieces
½ cup + 2 tablespoons whole milk, divided
½ cup water
Salt and freshly ground white pepper to taste
2 cups all-purpose flour
4 large eggs, room temperature, divided
1-½ cups gruyere, grated, divided (or comte)

Preheat oven to 400 degrees. In a saucepan add butter, one half cup milk, water, salt, and pepper. Bring to a boil over high heat until butter has melted completely, stirring constantly to prevent scorching. Remove from heat. Add flour all at once. Using a large wooden spoon, stir vigorously for 1 to 2 minutes or until mixture forms a thick dough and pulls away from the sides of the pan. Return pan to heat and cook for 1 minute, stirring constantly.

Remove from heat and set aside to cool for 5 minutes. Add eggs to dough, one at a time. (Beat eggs after each addition until completely incorporated into mixture and dough is smooth.) Add 1 cup of cheese and beat until well combined. Spoon tablespoon-size mounds of dough on to a non-stick baking sheet, about 1-inch apart. (You will need to use 2 baking sheets.) Using a pastry brush, lightly coat the tops of puffs with remaining two tablespoons of milk; then sprinkle the remaining ½ cup cheese on top, evenly dividing. Place one baking tray at a time in the oven on rack in the lower third of oven. Bake for 20 to 25 minutes or until puffs have doubled in size and are golden brown. Remove from oven and transfer to a wire rack to cool. Serve warm (or at room temperature). Makes about 3 dozen puffs.

'Inside Out' Crab Rangoon Dip with Wonton Chips

Named because the filling is used as a dip for fried wonton chips...thus the insides are outside. A real crowd pleaser.

DIP
1 pound cream cheese
4 ounces crab meat, fresh, shredded
    (or imitation crab meat)
¼ teaspoon Chinese 5-spice
½ teaspoon garlic powder
½ bunch green onions, washed, peeled,
    thinly sliced, for garnish

CHIPS
Vegetable oil, for frying
1 package wonton skins, thawed

For the dip, preheat oven to 350 degrees. In an electric mixer bowl add cream cheese and whip on high for 3 minutes or until fluffy. Add crab and both spices. Mix on medium until well combined. Transfer to an oven-safe baking dish. Cover tightly with aluminum foil. Place in oven and bake for 30 minutes. Remove cover and bake a bit longer until top is browned and bubbly. Remove from oven. Set aside to cool slightly. Top with green onions, for garnish.

For the chips, preheat a deep fryer (or large pot of oil) until instant-read thermometer reads 350 degrees. Place wonton skins on a clean cutting board. Using a sharp knife, cut from corner to corner to form triangle shapes. Carefully drop the wonton skins in hot oil, in small batches. Fry for 10 to 15 seconds. With a large slotted spoon, skim chips out of oil and transfer to a plate lined with paper towels to drain. Repeat process until all chips are cooked. Serve warm with warm crab dip. Makes 6 to 8 servings.

Etc.

Wonton wrappers are usually found in square packages in the produce section of the grocery store. They also make quick work of home-made ravioli. Just dollop your favorite filling, brush the edges with egg white to seal, then boil as you would pasta. Tip: When they float, they are done.

Sweet Potato Empanadas with Beef Picadillo Filling and Harissa Sauce

A unique and exceedingly tasty appetizer. Make them ahead of time and freeze them so they are ready when you need a wonderful "small plate." Prepare for applause.

SAUCE
2 large red bell peppers, roasted
2 cloves garlic, whole, peeled
2 whole jalapeno peppers (or other hot pepper),
   washed, stem removed
2 teaspoons ground cumin
1 teaspoon ground coriander
1 teaspoon ground caraway seeds
1 teaspoon salt
2 tablespoons olive oil
½ cup mayonnaise

FILLING
2 to 3 tablespoons olive oil
1 pound ground beef
½ large onion, peeled, chopped
2 cloves garlic, peeled, minced
2 tablespoons dried cranberries (or raisins)
2 tablespoons almonds, unsalted, roasted, chopped
2 tablespoons green olives (or capers), chopped
Salt and freshly ground black pepper to taste
1 tablespoon ground cumin
1 tablespoon ground coriander
¼ cup cilantro (or parsley), fresh, washed, chopped
1 large egg, lightly beaten

PASTRY
4 cups all-purpose flour plus more for rolling
2 cups cornmeal
2 teaspoons salt
1 pound butter, unsalted, cold
2 cups sweet potato puree, chilled
   (See note this page)
1 large egg white, beaten

For the sauce, in a food processor add red peppers, garlic, hot peppers, cumin, coriander, caraway seeds, and salt. Pulse until mixture is consistency of paste. While processor is running, slowly add oil and continue to blend until mixture is smooth. Turn off processor and add mayonnaise. Pulse mixture until smooth. Set aside.

For the filling, in a skillet heat oil. Add beef, onion and garlic. Sauté until beef is no longer pink, stirring occasionally to prevent burning. Remove from heat and set aside to cool. Add cranberries, almonds, olives, salt, pepper, cumin, coriander, and cilantro. Stir to combine well. Set aside.

For the pastry, in a food processor add flour, cornmeal, salt, and butter. Pulse until pieces of dough form to the size of a pea. Add puree and yolk. Continue to pulse until dough is moistened throughout. Transfer dough to a bowl and cover with plastic wrap. Place in refrigerator to chill for an hour. Remove from refrigerator and set aside until dough is pliable and able to be rolled out. Transfer dough to a lightly floured countertop (or pastry cloth). Using a rolling pin dusted with flour, roll dough out to 1/8-inch thickness. Using a round cookie cutter, cut dough into 3-inch rounds and transfer to a baking sheet.

Preheat oven to 350 degrees. To assemble empanadas, place one tablespoon of the filling into the center of each dough round. Using a pastry brush (or your fingers), paint edges with beaten egg. Fold dough over filling and pinch (or press with the tines of a fork) to seal edges. (Make sure that edges are completely sealed so that the filling doesn't bubble out when baking.) Place in oven and bake for 15 minutes or until golden brown. Remove from oven and transfer to a serving platter. Serve warm with Harissa Sauce for dipping. Makes 16 to 20 empanadas.

Moroccan Market Spicy Roasted Nuts

An unusual spiced nut that will keep your guests guessing...all the while with their fingers in the bowl.

Spray oil, for baking sheet
3 to 5 cups pecans, whole, unsalted (or walnuts,
    cashews, or shelled peanuts, or any combination
    of any of these nuts)
2 large egg whites, beaten until foamy
2 tablespoon ras el hanout (Moroccan curry powder)
1 tablespoon curry powder
1 teaspoon ground cumin
1 teaspoon cayenne pepper
2 teaspoons kosher salt

Preheat oven to 350 degrees and lightly spray a large rimmed baking sheet with oil. In a large bowl add nuts, egg whites, ras el hanout, curry, cumin, cayenne, and salt. Using a large wooden spoon, gently toss mixture until all nuts are well coated. Pour nut mixture onto the baking sheet and spread nuts out to a single layer. Place in oven and roast for 15 to 20 minutes or until fragrant and crisp, turning nuts halfway through baking. Remove from oven and set aside to cool on the baking sheet. Serve room temperature. Makes 3 to 5 cups.

Etc.

"Ras el hanout" is a mixture of spices that comes from Morocco in North Africa and can be found in the United States in specialty spice stores or ethnic markets. The Arabic definition is "head of the shop" meaning that all of the spices in the blend consist of the very best the vendor has to offer. The mixture of spices can vary from vendor to vendor with cinnamon, ground chili peppers, paprika, turmeric, coriander and cloves being the most common ingredients.

"Secret Ingredient" Spinach Dip

This recipe comes courtesy of one of our long-time instructors, Mari Ruck. Once students find out that the "secret ingredient" is tofu, they are amazed! This recipe is a great one to serve friends and family just to see if they know they're eating tofu. Go figure!

1 (10-½ ounce) package silken tofu, drained
   (found in the refrigerated section in
   major grocery stores)
½ package dry onion soup mix or to taste
½ cup mayonnaise
2 cloves garlic, peeled, chopped
1 (10-ounce) package frozen chopped spinach,
   thawed, thoroughly drained
¼ cup green onions, peeled, chopped
1 (8-ounce) can water chestnuts, drained

In a food processor, add tofu and blend for 2 minutes or until smooth. Add soup mix, mayonnaise, and garlic. Blend until smooth. Add spinach and blend just until combined. Add onions and water chestnuts. Pulse mixture until chunky. Transfer to a bowl and cover with a sheet of plastic wrap. Place in refrigerator for at least 1 hour. (Dip may be made up to 8 hours in advance.) Serve chilled. Makes about 2-1/2 cups.

Etc.

Tofu has a bland, slightly nutty flavor that gives it a chameleon-like capability to take on the flavor of the food or spices with which it's cooked. The word "silken" on the tofu package tells you that it's the one to choose when you want smooth and creamy results, such as for dips, puddings and cheesecakes.

Truffled Lentil Spoons
with Bacon Vinaigrette

Any Asian market will carry the china or plastic soup spoons with the flat bottom that sit by themselves nicely. Just mound a bit of this tasty cold salad in the spoon and let your guests pick one up and enjoy. An unusual presentation for a really tasty little bit of happiness.

TRUFFLE VINAIGRETTE
3 black truffles, fresh (found in specialty food stores)
½ cup truffle juice, plus 2 tablespoons
   (found in specialty food stores)
2 tablespoons sherry vinegar
1 tablespoon Dijon mustard
½ lemon, freshly juiced
½ cup white truffle oil (found in specialty food stores)
Salt and freshly ground black pepper to taste

BACON VINAIGRETTE
¼ cup almond oil
¼ cup olive oil
¾ cup sliced almonds, toasted
2 tablespoons Champagne vinegar
Salt and freshly ground black pepper to taste

LENTILS
¼ cup orange lentils, cooked, warm
¼ cup black lentils, cooked, warm
¼ cup French green lentils, cooked, warm
3 tablespoons truffle vinaigrette
Salt and freshly ground black pepper to taste
3 tablespoons bacon vinaigrette
12 to 18 long-handled decorative Asian soup spoons

12 to 18 sprigs chervil (or flat-leaf parsley),
   fresh, washed, dried, for garnish

Etc.

Appetizers served on single portion tasting spoons are the newest craze in entertaining. Individual spoons are a creative way to give your guests bite-size custom hors d'oeuvres that they can enjoy while mingling with the other guests. And clean up is a snap!

For the truffle vinaigrette, in a blender add truffles, truffle juice, vinegar, mustard, and juice. Puree until smooth. With the motor running, remove the plastic center on blender lid and slowly add oil in a steady, thin stream. Blend until emulsified. Transfer vinaigrette to a small glass (or ceramic bowl) and season with salt and pepper. Stir to combine and set aside. (Refrigerate remaining vinaigrette in an air-tight non-reactive container for up to 2 weeks. Whisk well before each use.)

For the bacon vinaigrette, in a glass measuring cup with a spout add almond oil and olive oil. Set aside. In a blender add almonds and vinegar. Puree until smooth and paste-like. With the blender running, remove the plastic center on lid and slowly add the oils in a slow, steady stream. Blend until well incorporated. Transfer to a small glass (or ceramic) bowl and season with salt and pepper. Stir to combine and set aside. (Remaining vinaigrette may be stored in an air-tight non-reactive container for up to 2 weeks. Whisk to mix well before each use.)

For the lentils, in a medium-size bowl add all lentils and truffle vinaigrette. Using a large wooden spoon, gently stir to combine until well coated. Add salt and pepper. Stir to combine and set aside.

To serve, scoop 2 tablespoons of the lentil mixture and place onto the end of a decorative Asian soup spoon. Set each spoon on a small dessert plate or place several decoratively on a platter. Quickly whisk the bacon vinaigrette in the bowl to re-mix. Drizzle over and around the "truffles", evenly dividing. Add a sprig of chervil on the side, for garnish. Makes 12 to 18 servings.

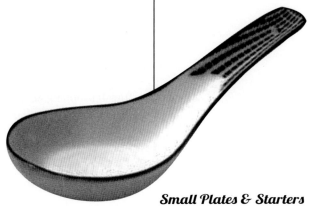

White-Bean and Swiss Chard Bruschetta

This recipe is an extremely healthy way to entertain. Your guests won't know that they are getting loads of nutrients.

BRUSCHETTA
44 (¼-inch thick) slices baguette bread, diagonally cut
3 tablespoons olive oil

DIP
5 tablespoons olive oil, divided
2 small onions, peeled, finely chopped
12 cloves garlic, fresh, peeled, minced
4 cups white beans, cooked, rinsed (such as cannellini)
4 teaspoons thyme, fresh, washed, minced
Salt and freshly ground black pepper to taste
6 cups Swiss chard, fresh, washed, cleaned, chopped
1-½ tablespoons white truffle oil

For the bruschetta, preheat oven to 400 degrees. On a large baking sheet add baguette slices and arrange in a single layer. With a pastry brush, lightly coat both sides of bread slices with oil, evenly dividing. Place in oven and bake for 8 minutes or until bread is lightly browned, turning once halfway through baking. Remove from oven and transfer to a large serving platter. Set aside.

For the dip, in a large skillet heat 3 tablespoons of oil over low heat. Add onion and garlic and cook for 5 minutes or until onion softens, stirring constantly. Add beans and cook another 3 minutes or until heated through, stirring constantly. Transfer mixture into a food processor (or blender) and puree until smooth. With the motor still running, add remaining 2 tablespoons oil in a slow, steady stream and mix until emulsified. Transfer mixture to a large bowl. Add thyme, salt, and pepper. Stir to combine well. Set aside (in the food processor bowl) in a warm place. Using a paper towel, wipe out the same skillet and set on stove over medium-high heat. Add chard. Using large tongs, gently toss until wilted. Immediately transfer chard to a large colander to cool slightly. Using hands, squeeze out any excess liquid. Add the chard and truffle oil to the bean mixture in the food processor. Blend for 20 seconds or until well combined. Transfer topping mixture into a bowl and set aside. To serve, top each bread slice with dollop of the bean dip, evenly dividing between all slices. Serve immediately. Makes 44 bruschetta.

Etc.

Swiss chard is one of the healthiest greens on the planet. Its large, dense, green leaves contain large amounts of antioxidants and anti-inflammatory benefits. Don't wash until just before use. Run cold water over the chard (do not soak) and remove any leaves that are brown or have holes. Stack the leaves and using a sharp knife, slice them into 1-inch slices from the outside in, just until you reach the middle and discard the tough stems.

Lesson Two

Salads & Dressings

Asian Noodle Salad with Spicy Soy Dressing

Endive and Apple Salad with Toasted Walnuts and Champagne Vinaigrette

Fig Balsamic Vinaigrette

Miso-Sesame Vinaigrette

Ruthie's Spinach Salad

Simple Lime-Cilantro Slaw

Salad Greens with Baked Goat Cheese and Port-Pancetta Dressing

Strawberry Balsamic Vinaigrette

Tandoori Chicken Salad

Tuscan Panzanella Salad

Asian Noodle Salad with Spicy Soy Dressing

We have been preparing this dish at The Culinary Center since we opened in May 1998 and it's still one of the most popular with our guests. The glory of this salad is that it's hard to mess up and tastes wonderful whether served warm, at room temperature, or cold.

DRESSING
¾-inch piece ginger root, fresh, peeled, sliced, finely chopped
2 jalapeno peppers (or more, if desired), washed, cored, seeded, finely diced
2 cloves garlic, fresh, peeled, finely chopped
2 teaspoons sugar
Salt and freshly ground pepper to taste
¼ cup rice wine vinegar
½ cup soy sauce
¼ cup peanut oil (or vegetable oil)
2 tablespoons sesame oil

SALAD
8 ounces Chinese thin egg noodles (or thin spaghetti), cooked, drained well, warm
6 ounces snow peas, fresh, washed, trimmed, steamed until crisp tender, cut into diagonal slices
¾ pound baby shrimp, fresh (or frozen and thawed), cooked
4 scallions, washed, peeled, cut into diagonal slices
½ cup peanuts, roasted, unsalted, coarsely chopped, divided
1 small bunch cilantro, fresh, washed, dried, leaves stripped from stems, coarsely chopped, divided

For the dressing, in a bowl add ginger, peppers, garlic, sugar, salt, pepper, and vinegar. Whisk well to combine. Pour in soy sauce and whisk to combine. Gradually pour in peanut and sesame oils, while whisking, so that the sauce emulsifies and thickens slightly. Set aside.

For the salad, in a large salad bowl add warm noodles. Briskly whisk dressing and immediately pour it over the noodles. Using salad tongs, toss salad together until well coated.

Etc.

This can be a very versatile salad by varying the content of ingredients. Depending on how we feel, one day it may contain lots of vegetables and on another day we replace the shrimp for grilled chicken. For the latter, we make double the amount of dressing to use to marinate boneless, skinless chicken breasts for at least 2 hours. Then grill, slice on the diagonal and fan out over the top of the salad. Either way, this is a delicious salad!

Set aside to marinate at room temperature for at least one hour for flavors to blend together. Add snow peas, shrimp, scallions, and two-thirds of both the peanuts and cilantro. Using salad tongs, toss salad together thoroughly. To serve, transfer salad to a large serving platter. Top with remaining peanuts and cilantro, for garnish. Serve immediately. Makes 4 servings.

Endive and Apple Salad with Toasted Walnuts and Champagne Vinaigrette

This is a good winter salad because of its ingredients are readily available at that time, but feel free to enjoy this elegant combination year-round.

VINAIGRETTE
3 tablespoon champagne vinegar
¼ cup walnut oil
Salt and freshly ground black pepper to taste

SALAD
2 large apples (preferably Gala), washed,
*   quartered, cored, thinly sliced*
2 tablespoons lemon juice, freshly squeezed
2 heads endive leaves, washed, dried
½ cups walnuts, whole, toasted

For the vinaigrette, in a small bowl add vinegar and oil. Whisk together thoroughly. Add salt and pepper. Stir to combine. Set aside.

For the salad, in a medium salad bowl add apples and juice. Using a large spoon, stir to coat the apples thoroughly to prevent browning. Set aside. To serve, on 4 individual salad plates add one to two endive leaves as desired. Top each leaf with one-quarter of the apple mixture. Sprinkle the walnuts decoratively around each plate and dress with vinaigrette. Serve immediately. Makes 4 salads.

Etc.

To toast walnuts, preheat oven to 350 degrees. Arrange walnuts on a baking sheet in a single layer and place in oven. Toast for 10 minutes or until you get a strong smell of the nuts roasting. Watch nuts closely as they will burn in an instant. Once the nuts have cooled, they may be kept in a sealed container in the freezer for up to 2 months.

Fig Balsamic Vinaigrette

Tired of making the same old salad dressings?
Try this one and you'll have a new "go to" recipe.

FIG BALSAMIC VINEGAR
1 cup balsamic vinegar
½ cup dried figs, stems removed

VINAIGRETTE
1 cup Fig Balsamic Vinegar
2 cloves garlic, fresh, roasted, peeled
2 cups olive oil
1 teaspoon kosher (or sea) salt
½ teaspoon freshly ground black pepper

For the fig vinegar, in a blender add vinegar and figs. Blend on high for 2 minutes. Set aside. (May be made ahead and stored in an air-tight container.)

For the vinaigrette, in a blender add fig vinegar and garlic. Blend on high for 10 seconds. Whiles blender is running, slowly add oil in a steady stream until all is incorporated. Transfer to a bowl. Add salt and pepper. Stir to combine. (Vinaigrette may be kept in refrigerator for up to 2 weeks.) Serve cold or at room temperature. Makes 3 cups.

Etc.

You can find dried figs year-round. Fresh figs are a bit harder to find as they are only in season from June through September. If using fresh figs, double the amounts called for.

Miso-Sesame Vinaigrette

Our most requested dish in our popular "Dinners on Demand™" program with its chef-prepared dishes for sale. Our staff calls this dressing "Me So Sexy" Vinaigrette. Seriously, it is amazingly addictive.

½ cup rice wine vinegar
¼ cup water
6 tablespoons white miso paste (found in Asian
    markets or in more major grocery stores)
¼ cup sugar
2 tablespoons peanut butter, creamy
1 tablespoon ginger root, fresh, peeled, chopped
1 teaspoon garlic, chopped
1 jalapeno pepper (or serrano), washed,
    halved, seeded, minced
2 teaspoons pure sesame oil
2 teaspoons Dijon mustard
1 cup canola oil
2 teaspoons sesame seeds, toasted

In a blender add vinegar, water, miso paste, sugar, peanut butter, ginger, garlic, jalapeno, sesame oil, and mustard. Puree until smooth. With machine running, slowly stream canola oil in and blend until incorporated. Transfer vinaigrette to a bowl. Add sesame seeds and gently stir to combine. (If mixture seems too thick, add water, a little at a time, until vinaigrette can be poured easily.) Cover bowl with plastic wrap (or lid) and refrigerate until needed. (Vinaigrette will keep for up to 3 weeks in refrigerator. If not used right away, it will need to be stirred (or shaken) to combine ingredients.) Serve cold. Makes 3 cups.

Etc.

Miso is a Japanese seasoning used in many traditional dishes and most likely the taste in this recipe that makes it so hard to resist. It is a thick paste and can be quite salty but depending on the ingredients and fermentation process, can also be found in sweet, earthy, and savory varieties. White miso consists of soybeans that have been fermented with rice and has a sweeter taste making it perfect for light salad dressings.

Ruthie's Spinach Salad

A classic time-honored salad that is just the thing for picnics and tail-gate parties.

DRESSING
1 cup salad oil
½ cup sugar
½ cup red wine vinegar
3 to 4 cloves garlic, fresh, peeled, finely minced
½ teaspoon salt
½ teaspoon paprika
¼ teaspoon freshly ground black pepper
¼ teaspoon cayenne pepper

SALAD
8 cups spinach, fresh, stems removed, thoroughly washed and dried
1 cup dried cranberries (or dried cherries)
4 ounces feta cheese, crumbled
1 medium red onion, peeled, thinly sliced
4 to 6 slices bacon, cooked, drained, crumbled
½ cup almonds, toasted, slivered

For the dressing, in a container with a tight fitting lid add oil, sugar, vinegar, garlic, salt, paprika, black pepper, and cayenne pepper. Cover and shake well to mix well. (Dressing may be made up to one week ahead of time and stored in refrigerator.) Set aside.

To assemble salad, in a large salad bowl add spinach, cranberries, cheese, onions, bacon, and almonds. Pour dressing over top and toss to combine. Serve immediately. Makes 6 servings.

Simple
Lime-Cilantro Slaw

This slaw has been served by my Mom at almost every holiday meal that I can recall so it only makes sense that I would want to share this family tradition. That's what cooks do, don't they?

6 cups green cabbage, fresh, washed, thinly sliced
¾ cup cilantro, fresh, washed, coarsely chopped
1 teaspoon coarse sea salt
¼ teaspoon freshly ground black pepper
¼ cup lime juice plus more to taste, freshly squeezed
2 tablespoons orange juice plus more to taste,
   freshly squeezed
1 tablespoon sugar (optional)
3 tablespoons extra virgin olive oil

In a large serving bowl add cabbage, cilantro, salt, and pepper. Set aside. In a small bowl add lime juice, orange juice, sugar, and oil. Whisk to combine thoroughly. Pour dressing over the cabbage mix. Using tongs (or large spoon) toss slaw together until well coated. Taste and add more lime or orange juice, if needed. Serve cold. Makes 6 servings.

Etc.

Slaw, which is slang for coleslaw, is a cold salad that uses shredded cabbage as the base and tossed with either a mayonnaise or vinegar dressing. This popular salad is a staple at backyard barbecues, picnics, potlucks...and Laiben family gatherings!

Salad Greens with Baked Goat Cheese and Port-Pancetta Dressing

This is my "go to" salad for entertaining. The presentation is lovely and the flavor combination is over the top. It is always a hit!

DRESSING
1-¼ cups dried tart cherries (or dried cranberries)
½ cup tawny port wine
5 ounces pancetta (or bacon), chopped
2 shallots, peeled, minced
1 clove garlic, peeled, minced
⅓ cup olive oil
¼ cup red wine vinegar
2 teaspoons sugar
Salt and freshly ground black pepper to taste

CHEESE
½ cup breadcrumbs
1 (5-½ ounce) log soft goat cheese, fresh,
    cut into ½-inch thick slices (such as Montrachet)

SALAD
8 to 12 cups mixed salad greens, washed, dried
½ cup pine nuts, toasted

For the dressing, in a small heavy saucepan add cherries and port. Bring to a boil over medium heat. Remove from heat and set aside for about 15 minutes or until cherries swell in size. Meanwhile, in a large heavy skillet over medium-low heat, add pancetta and cook for 8 minutes or until crisp. Add shallots and garlic.Cook for an additional 2 minutes, stirring constantly to prevent burning. Add oil, then vinegar and sugar. Stir dressing until the sugar is completely dissolved. Add cherry mixture, salt, and pepper. Stir to combine. Set aside in skillet until ready to use. (Dressing can be made 2 hours in advance and set aside in the skillet at room temperature.)

For the cheese, preheat oven to 350 degrees. In a shallow bowl add breadcrumbs. Place cheese slices in crumbs and press to coat evenly on both sides. Transfer to a baking sheet and place in oven. Bake for 10 minutes or until cheese warms. Remove from oven and set aside.

For the salad, in a large salad bowl add greens and pine nuts. Pour the warmed dressing over top of salad. Using salad tongs, gently toss to coat all greens. Top with the warm goat cheese. Serve immediately. Makes 6 to 8 servings.

Strawberry Balsamic Vinaigrette

The combination of strawberries and balsamic will make your salads pop with flavor. Your new top-shelf vinaigrette! You're welcome.

½ cup strawberry preserves (preferably organic)
½ cup white wine vinegar
1 shallot, caramelized
2 cloves garlic, whole, roasted, peeled
2 cups olive oil
1 teaspoon dry tarragon (or 3 teaspoons fresh)
½ teaspoon kosher salt
¼ teaspoon freshly ground white pepper

In a blender add preserves, vinegar, shallot, and garlic. Blend for 30 seconds to mix. Remove the blender cap. While motor is running, slowly stream oil into blender and mix until combined. Transfer vinaigrette to a bowl. Add tarragon, salt, and pepper. Whisk to combine. Cover with plastic wrap (or lid) and place in refrigerator until ready to serve. (Vinaigrette can be kept in refrigerator for up to 2 months.) Serve cold. Makes approximately 3 cups.

Etc.

Most seasoned cooks – both professional and home – know the secret to a great salad is to make the dressing from scratch and vinaigrettes are by far the easiest to throw together. A simple vinaigrette is an oil-and-vinegar combination –usually 3 parts oil to 1 part vinegar - seasoned with salt and pepper. You can personalize it with flavored or infused vinegars and oils, etc.

Tandoori Chicken Salad

Turn your chicken salad upside down with this exotic and extremely tasty version.

MARINADE
2 cloves garlic, fresh, peeled, minced
1 cup onion, diced
1 (1-inch) piece ginger root, fresh, peeled, chopped (or grated)
2 tablespoons lemon juice, freshly squeezed
1 cup plain yogurt
½ tablespoons salt
¼ cup olive oil (or vegetable oil)
1 tablespoon turmeric
1 tablespoon cayenne pepper
½ tablespoon ground curry powder
½ tablespoon ground coriander
½ tablespoon ground cinnamon
½ teaspoon paprika
Pinch of ground cloves
Pinch of allspice
1 teaspoon saffron (optional)

2 to 3 pounds chicken breasts, skinless, boneless
1 large red bell pepper, washed, seeded, finely diced
2 to 3 stalks celery, washed, finely diced
1 small red onion, peeled, finely diced
½ cup cilantro (or parsley), fresh, chopped
Salt and freshly ground black pepper to taste
1 cup mayonnaise (preferably homemade)
Salt and freshly ground black pepper to taste

For the marinade, in a food processor (or blender) add garlic, onion, ginger, lemon juice, yogurt, salt, oil, turmeric, cayenne pepper, curry powder, coriander, cinnamon, paprika, cloves, allspice and saffron. Process until marinade is fairly smooth. Set aside.

In a non-reactive baking dish add chicken. Pour marinade over top and cover dish with plastic wrap. Place in refrigerator to marinate at least 8 hours or overnight. When ready to cook, preheat oven to 350 degrees. Remove from refrigerator. Transfer chicken from marinade onto a baking sheet. Place in oven and bake for 15 minutes or until chicken is springy when pressed with fingertips. Remove from oven and set aside to cool. Transfer chicken to a cutting board. Using a sharp knife, finely dice chicken. Set aside.

To assemble salad, in a large salad bowl add chicken, red peppers, celery, onion, cilantro, salt and papper. Using a large spoon, stir to combine. Add mayonnaise and stir to coat salad completely. Adjust seasonings. Evenly divide salad onto individual salad plates. Serve immediately. Makes 10 to 12 servings.

Etc.

Lavosh crackers or pita bread make the perfect accompaniment.

Tuscan Panzanella Salad

In the Tuscany region of Italy, where bread is "king," this dish is a staple. Bread is never wasted. Even when it's stale, it's used to create simple and delicious dishes, including soups and this great salad. Any kind of stale bread will work but hearty country bread is preferred. Balsamic vinegar can be substituted for the red wine vinegar which will add a whole new dimension to the salad.

4 (¾-inch) slices Italian bread, stale,
  cut or turn into small, rough chunks
3 to 4 cups water
1 clove garlic, peeled, halved
4 large tomatoes, vine-ripened, washed,
  cored, cut into 1-inch pieces
½ pound Romaine lettuce (or Swiss chard,
  spinach or any other sturdy lettuce or green),
  washed, dried, torn into bite-size pieces
1 large red onion, peeled, thinly sliced
1 medium cucumber, peeled,
  cut into ¼-inch slices
2 to 4 tablespoons red wine vinegar
¼ cup extra virgin olive oil
¼ cup Italian flat-leaf parsley, fresh, washed,
  dried, finely chopped
2 tablespoons basil, fresh, stems removed,
  washed, dried, finely chopped
2 tablespoons oregano, fresh, washed,
  dried, chopped
Salt and freshly ground black pepper to taste

Etc.

This recipe calls for soaking the bread in water; but, if you don't have time to do so or your bread is not that stale, you may skip that step. The salad will still turn out wonderfully!

In a medium bowl add bread and enough water to just cover the bread. Set aside for about 5 minutes to allow the water to soak into the bread. Meanwhile, in a large salad bowl rub exposed portions of garlic inside the entire bowl. Discard garlic. Using your hands, remove bread from bowl, one fistful at a time, and squeeze out as much water as possible; then place in bowl. Using a fork, break bread apart into smaller pieces. Add tomatoes, lettuce, onion, cucumber, vinegar, oil, parsley, basil, and oregano. Using salad tongs, gently toss all ingredients until well combined. Add salt and pepper and lightly toss to combine. Divide salad evenly among 4 individual salad plates. Serve immediately. Makes 4 servings.

Lesson Three

Soups

Butternut Squash Soup

Curried Carrot Soup

Dublin Coddle "Codal Dublinneach"

Leek and Asparagus Soup with Boursin Cheese

Lentil Soup with Morrocan Spices

Low-Fat Black Bean Soup

Potage Saint-Germain

Spicy Corn Chowder

Tomato Cognac Soup

Tuscan Bean Soup

Butternut Squash Soup

A beautiful and complex soup that is perfect for cool weather.

3 medium (about 10" long) butternut squash
5 tablespoons olive oil, divided
2 medium yellow onions, peeled, diced
3 stalks celery, washed, diced
2 tablespoons garlic, fresh, peeled, chopped
1-½ cups sherry wine
2 bay leaves
1 tablespoon French thyme, fresh, chopped
2 tablespoons ginger root, fresh, peeled, diced
2 tablespoons curry powder
1 tablespoon cracked black pepper
1 gallon vegetable stock
1-½ cups heavy cream
2 tablespoons Worcestershire sauce
   (Lea & Perrins preferred)
2 tablespoons Louisiana brand Hot Sauce
1 tablespoon dried ground ginger
1 tablespoon salt

Using a knife make a few slashes in squash to release steam as squash is roasting. Rub squash with 1 tablespoon oil and roast in oven at 350 degrees until just tender about 30 minutes. Let cool to the touch and then peel and cut flesh into chunks. Set aside.

In a large stockpot heat remaining 4 tablespoons oil over medium-high heat. Add onions, celery and garlic. Sauté until onions are translucent, stirring constantly. Add sherry, bay leaves, thyme, and fresh ginger. Cook until reduced by one-half, stirring occasionally. Add curry powder, black pepper, stock and reserved squash and cook until ingredients are tender. Remove bay leaf. Blend with an immersion blender. Add cream, Worcestershire, hot sauce, dried ginger and salt. Simmer another 15 minutes allowing flavors to meld. Serve warm. Makes 6 to 8 servings.

Curried Carrot Soup

"I'm simple, easy and fabulous!"...that's what this unique soup would say if it could talk. Let me go ahead and say it then,"This soup speaks for itself!"

3 tablespoons olive oil
3 large onions, peeled, diced
6 cloves garlic, fresh, peeled, minced
1 teaspoon curry powder
1 teaspoon garam masala
1 teaspoon ground coriander
1 teaspoon mustard seed, whole
¼ teaspoon cayenne pepper
Salt and freshly ground pepper to taste
10 large carrots, peeled, ends removed,
    cut into 1-inch chunks
2 quarts vegetable stock
3 tablespoons honey (optional)
1 quart heavy whipping cream
Cilantro, fresh, for garnish
Croutons, for garnish

In a large stockpot heat oil over high heat. Add onions and garlic and sauté for 5 to 8 minutes or until onions are soft and translucent, stirring constantly to prevent scorching. Add curry, garam masala, coriander, mustard seed, cayenne, salt, and pepper. Sauté for 1 to 2 minutes to blend spices in, stirring constantly to prevent burning. Add carrots and stock. Reduce heat to low and simmer soup until carrots are tender. Add honey and stir to combine. Remove from heat and set aside to cool for 30 minutes.

In a blender (or food processor) transfer soup and puree until smooth. Return pureed soup to pot. Add cream and heat thoroughly, stirring constantly. (Do not allow soup to boil during this step.) Remove from heat.

To serve, ladle soup into individual soup bowls. Top with cilantro and croutons, dividing evenly, for garnish. Serve warm. Makes 8 servings.

Etc.

Garam masala is a blend of dry-roasted ground spices that add a "warmth" to a dish. It generally includes black pepper, cinnamon, cloves, coriander, cumin, cardamom, dried chilies, fennel, mace, nutmeg and other spices. It is usually added toward the end of the cooking for a recipe or sprinkled over the surface of food just before serving. This very interesting spice blend can be found in specialty stores selling Indian products and sometimes in major grocery stores.

Dublin Coddle
("Codal Dublinneach")

This is Irish heritage cooking at its finest. I like to prepare this dish and then ask my guests to guess the secret ingredient. Their eyes always widen when I tell them it's hard cider. It's an amazing hearty soup that also freezes well. And c'mon.....it has bacon in it, you can't go wrong!

1 pound bacon, cut into thin strips
2 pounds pork sausages, cut into large chunks
2 large onions, peeled, rough cut
2 cloves garlic, fresh, peeled, chopped
4 large potatoes, washed, skin on,
*   cut into large chunks*
4 carrots, fresh, peeled, ends removed, thickly sliced
1 to 2 bottles hard cider (or apple wine or apple cider)
1 herb bundle, tied with a string
*   (rosemary, parsley, thyme, etc.)*
Freshly ground black pepper to taste
Fresh parsley, washed, chopped, for garnish

Preheat a large heavy-bottomed stockpot over medium-high heat. Add bacon and fry until crisp, stirring often to prevent burning. Using a large slotted spoon, lift the bacon out (leave fat in the skillet) and set the bacon aside.

In the same stockpot add sausages and brown until deep golden brown. Using a large slotted spoon, lift the sausages out and set aside. In the same stockpot, add onions, garlic and cook until translucent, stirring constantly. Add the bacon and sausages back to the stockpot. Add potatoes and carrots. Add enough cider to completely cover the meat and vegetables. (You can also use a combination of hard cider and water.) Add the herb bundle by burying in the middle of the mixture, using a large spoon. Add pepper. Cook for 1-½ hours over low or moderate heat, stirring occasionally. (Do not boil. "Coddle" it!) (At this point, you could also place all the ingredients in a slow cooker and cook on low for 6 to 8 hours.) Remove from heat.

To serve, ladle the coddle into large soup bowls. Sprinkle with parsley, for garnish. Serve warm. Makes servings for 6 very hungry Irishmen.

Leek and Asparagus Soup with Boursin Cheese

A simple, yet elegant addition to your entertaining menus.

4 tablespoons butter (or olive oil), divided
1 shallot, peeled, finely chopped
2 leeks, outer leaves removed, washed, trimmed,
*   thinly sliced*
1 pound asparagus, fresh, stems trimmed,
*   cut into thirds, reserving tips, for garnish*
1 teaspoon curry powder or more to taste (optional)
Salt and freshly ground black pepper to taste
4 cups chicken stock
½ cup light cream (optional)
5 ounces Boursin cheese, for garnish
1 bunch chives, washed, chopped, for garnish

In a large saucepan melt 2 tablespoons butter. Add shallots and leeks. Saute for 3 minutes or until the white part of the leeks are opaque and green parts are brightly colored. Add asparagus (not tips), curry, salt, and pepper. Cook for another 3 minutes, stirring constantly to prevent burning. Add stock and simmer for 15 minutes or until asparagus is very tender. Meanwhile, in a small pan add remaining 2 tablespoons butter and asparagus tips. Saute for 3 to 5 minutes or until tender. Set aside. Add cream to soup base and correct the seasonings. Heat on low until heated through. (For a more refined dish, puree all ingredients in a food processor. To puree right in the soup pot, use a hand-held immersion blender.) To serve, ladle soup into individual soup bowls. Top with asparagus tips, a dollop of Boursin cheese and sprinkle with chives, for garnish. Serve warm. Makes 4 servings.

Etc.

Boursin cheese is trademarked brand of Gournay cheese and has a soft, creamy texture similar to cream cheese. When using a food processor to puree any ingredients which have been cooked, be sure to let them cool before processing. If you don't, the result may very well be a Mount Vesuvius-like disaster on your kitchen ceiling and walls!

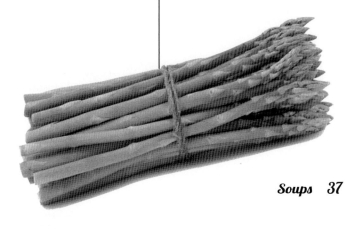

Lentil Soup with Moroccan Spices

This could well become one of your new favorite soups. Chef Gary Hild has taught with us since we opened and we can always count on him for exceptional recipes.

BOUQUET GARNI
1 (6- to 8-inch square) cheesecloth
1 rib celery
1 sprig rosemary, fresh, washed
1 sprig parsley, fresh, washed
Kitchen string

SOUP
½ cup olive oil
2 cups celery, diced
2 cups onions, diced
2 cups carrots, diced
¼ cup garlic, fresh, peeled, minced
2 tablespoons paprika
2 tablespoons tumeric
2 tablespoons ground cumin
5 cups lentils, uncooked
5 quarts chicken stock
3 cups heavy cream
Salt and freshly ground black pepper to taste

For the bouquet garni, on a piece of cheesecloth add celery, rosemary, and parsley. Gather up the sides of the cheesecloth to form a pouch (or bundle) around the celery and herbs. Tightly tie a piece of kitchen string around top to seal. Set aside.

For the soup, in a large stockpot heat oil over medium heat. Add celery, onions, carrots, and garlic. Sauté for 5 minutes or until vegetables are translucent, stirring frequently to prevent burning. Add the paprika, tumeric, and cumin and continue to sauté for an additional 2 minutes, stirring constantly. Add lentils, stock and bouquet garni. Cook for 40 minutes or until the lentils are soft and tender. Remove from heat. Using a large slotted spoon, skim out the bouquet garni pouch and discard. Add cream, salt, and pepper. Stir to combine. Serve warm. Makes 7 quarts of soup.

Low-Fat
Black Bean Soup

This soup is a great way to fill up without filling out! The base is black beans (also known as "turtle beans"), which are popular in Mexico and South America . They are available in grocery stores and can be found either canned or dried, usually under the name of "frijoles negros."

¾ cup dried black beans, sorted, washed, drained
Water, for cooking
2 teaspoons vegetable-flavored bouillon granules
Spray oil, for pan
1 cup onion, peeled, chopped
½ cup celery, washed, chopped
½ cup carrot, peeled, chopped
2 cloves garlic, fresh, peeled, minced
½ teaspoon ground cumin
¼ teaspoon freshly ground black pepper
2 tablespoons low-fat yogurt, for garnish
1 tablespoon chives, fresh, washed, minced,
    for garnish

In a medium saucepan on medium-high heat add beans and cover with water until about 2-inches above beans. Bring to a boil and cook for 2 minutes. Remove from heat and cover pan. Set aside for 1 hour. Place pan back on stovetop over medium-high heat. Stir in bouillon granules and bring to boil. Cover and reduce heat to simmer. Cook for 2 ½ hours or until beans are tender, stirring occasionally. Lightly spray skillet with oil and place on medium heat. Add onion, celery, carrot, and garlic. Cook for 5 minutes or until vegetables are soft, stirring frequently. Add to soup along with cumin, and pepper. Stir to combine well. Bring mixture to a boil. Reduce heat to low and simmer, uncovered, for 30 minutes, stirring occasionally. Remove from heat and set aside to cool slightly. Transfer soup to a blender (or food processor) and puree.

To serve, ladle soup into individual soup bowls. Top with a dollop of low-fat or non-fat yogurt and sprinkle with chives, for garnish. Serve warm. Makes 3 to 4 servings.

Etc.

Cumin is the dried fruit of a plant in the parsley family. It has a nutty-flavored, aromatic seed and is available in seed and ground form. Popular in Middle Eastern, Asian and Mediterranean cooking, cumin is an ingredient used in making curry and chili powders.

Potage Saint-Germain

Don't be fooled by the fancy French name for this lovely split pea soup. "Potage" in French means a thick creamy soup.

1 tablespoon butter, unsalted
½ cup leeks, fresh, washed, white part only,
    thinly sliced
¼ teaspoon salt
¼ teaspoon freshly ground black pepper
Pinch of sugar
2 cups peas, fresh, shelled (or tiny frozen peas)
1 cup romaine lettuce, shredded
2 tablespoons chervil, fresh, washed, chopped
6 cups chicken stock, divided (or vegetable)

Parsley sprigs, fresh, washed, for garnish

In a large saucepan melt butter over medium heat. Add leeks, salt, pepper, and sugar. Stir to combine. Cook for 5 minutes or until softened, stirring constantly. Add peas, lettuce, chervil, and 1 cup of the stock. Cover and cook for 5 minutes or until peas are tender. Remove from heat.

In a blender (or food processor) add warm liquid and remaining 5 cups stock, working in batches. Puree after each addition until very smooth. Strain each batch through a fine mesh sieve set over the same saucepan. Place saucepan back on medium heat and re-heat.

To serve, ladle equal portions of the soup into individual soup bowls. Garnish each with a sprig of parsley. Serve warm. Makes 4 to 6 servings.

Spicy Corn Chowder

In the height of summer, turn the ubiquitous ears of corn into this flavorful dish. Freeze a quart or two for those cool evenings when you long for the tastes of summer.

2 tablespoons butter, unsalted
1 large yellow onion, peeled, coarsely chopped
1 large shallot, minced
6 cups light cream (or "half and half")
8 ears corn, fresh, shucked, kernels removed,
    divided (or 3 cups frozen)
1 large red bell pepper, roasted, peeled,
    seeded, pureed (optional)
1 teaspoon ground cumin
1 teaspoon oregano, dried
1 jalapeno pepper, washed, minced, or more to taste
Salt and freshly ground black pepper to taste
2 tablespoons chives, fresh, washed,
    finely chopped, for garnish

Etc.

The two most common types of corn are sweet and field corn. The sweet variety is what you would enjoy on your dinner table while field corn is used as livestock feed. Specialty corns such as the blue variety are grown for their high levels of certain nutrients and colored corns have multi-colored kernels and are used mainly in decorations.

In a large saucepan melt butter over low to medium heat. Add onion and shallot and sauté for 5 minutes or until translucent, stirring frequently. Add cream and about three-fourths of the corn. Stir to mix and bring to a boil. Reduce heat to low and simmer, uncovered, for 10 minutes or until corn is tender and the liquid thickens slightly, stirring frequently to prevent scorching. Remove from heat.

Add pepper puree, cumin, oregano, jalapeno peppers, salt, and black pepper. Stir to combine and set aside to cool for 5 minutes. In a food processor fitted with a metal blade (or blender) add soup, in small batches. (You will need to place a strainer over the top of the food processor cup, add puree and then force liquid through the strainer by pressing the solids down with a large wooden spoon (discard solids). Puree liquid until well combined.

Return the chowder to the saucepan. Add remaining one-fourth of corn kernels. Simmer over low to medium heat for 5 minutes or until kernels are tender-crisp, stirring occasionally. Adjust seasonings. Remove from heat. To serve, ladle equal portions of soup into warmed soup bowls. Top with chives, for garnish. Serve warm. Makes 6 to 8 servings.

Tomato Cognac Soup

There is no question that this IS our favorite soup here at The Culinary Center. Simple, elegant and addictive.

6 pounds tomatoes, whole, canned with liquid
12 tablespoons butter, unsalted
2 large yellow onions, peeled, diced
2 tablespoons basil, dried
1 quart heavy cream
4 tablespoons brown sugar
¾ cup cognac
Salt and freshly ground pepper to taste
Parsley, fresh (or chives or hot croutons),
**   for garnish**

In a large mixing bowl add tomatoes. Using hands (or potato masher), squash tomatoes into smaller pieces. Set aside.

In a sauté pan melt butter. Add onions and sauté for 5 minutes or until soft but not brown. Add tomatoes, including their liquid, to pan. Add basil and stir to combine well. Bring mixture to a boil; then reduce heat and simmer, covered, for 20 minutes. Remove from heat and set aside to cool. Transfer mixture to a food processor and puree. Set aside.

In a small saucepan over medium heat, add cream and sugar and heat slightly, whisking often. Pour in tomato mixture. Stir to combine. Continue to cook soup until heated through but do not boil. Remove from heat.

Add cognac, salt, and pepper. Stir to combine. To serve, ladle soup into individual soup bowls. Top with parsley, for garnish. Serve warm. Makes 6 to 8 servings.

Etc.

Feel free to use fresh tomatoes in this recipe, if desired. Substitute 5 to 6 whole, peeled tomatoes for a 14-ounce can and 10 to 12 for a 28-ounce can.

Tuscan Bean Soup

This recipe is a staple of our "All Hands For Hunger™" interactive teambuilding model where local companies create freezers full of food for charities serving the underprivileged here in Kansas City. It's hearty, healthy and freezes well. Oh yes...it's delicious too!

1/8 pound bacon, chopped
1 tablespoon olive oil
1 cup carrots, washed, peeled, diced
1 cup onions, diced
1/2 cup celery, washed, diced
1 white potato, peeled, 1/4-inch dice
1-1/2 large red bell peppers, washed,
    seeded, medium dice
1-1/2 quarts white beans, cooked, drained
1-1/2 quarts water
1 cup whole tomatoes, canned,
    processed slightly in food processor (or blender)
2 teaspoons salt
3/4 teaspoon red pepper flakes
3/4 teaspoon freshly cracked black pepper
1/2 tablespoon rosemary, fresh, washed

In a 1-gallon stock pot add bacon and sauté over medium-high heat until lightly crisp, stirring constantly. Add oil, carrots, onions, celery, potato, and peppers and sauté until halfway tender, stirring constantly to prevent burning. Add beans, water, tomatoes, salt, red pepper flakes, black pepper, and rosemary. Stir to mix and bring to a boil.

Reduce heat to simmer and continue to cook for an additional 15 minutes. Remove from heat. To serve, ladle into individual soup bowls. Serve warm. Makes 4 quarts.

Etc.

Serve cornbread and honey butter alongside this soup for a full meal experience.

Lesson Four

Main Dishes

"All Hands For Hunger"™ Chicken Scallopini

Almond-Crusted Cod with Roasted Sweet Potatoes

Beer Braised Brisket

Chicken Spiedini with Amogia Sauce

Cowboy KC Strip Steak with Tobacco Onions

Grilled Lamb with Rosemary

Doris Laiben's Ultimate Eggplant Parmesan Casserole

Grilled Salmon with Fresh Corn and Tomato Sauté

Leek & Tomato Quiche

Mom's Holiday Brisket

Potato-Encrusted Tilapia Filets With Two Sauces

Pork Rack with Apricot Cognac Sauce

Tuscan-Style Strip Steaks

Shrimp in Garlic Cream with Mushrooms and Penne Pasta

"All Hands For Hunger"™ Chicken Scallopini

For a while we were creating this dish so much for our very popular "All Hands For Hunger"™ interactive cooking parties that we called ourselves The Kansas City Scallopini Center. Seriously, our program where companies bring their employees in to create freezers full of food for local charities means that the under-served and the needy eat very well. That makes EVERYONE involved feel great.

CHICKEN
½ cup olive oil
1 cup all-purpose flour
½ teaspoon salt
½ teaspoon freshly ground black pepper
4 (5-ounce) chicken breasts, boneless, skin off, pounded to ½-inch thick

SAUCE
1 shallot, peeled, large dice
1 cup button mushrooms, washed, dried, sliced thin
1 clove garlic, peeled, small dice
½ cup dry white wine (such as Chardonnay or Pinot Grigio)
1-½ cups chicken stock
6 Roma tomatoes, washed, ends trimmed, large dice
1 cup artichoke hearts (canned or jarred), drained, quartered
1 tablespoon parsley, fresh, washed, chopped
1 tablespoon oregano, fresh, washed, chopped
Salt and freshly ground white pepper to taste

ROUX
4 tablespoons butter, unsalted
⅓ cup all-purpose flour

4 servings linguini pasta, cooked

For the chicken, in a skillet heat oil over medium-high heat. In shallow pan add flour, salt, and pepper, Stir to combine. Place chicken in flour, one at a time, and dredge to cover completely. Immediately add chicken to skillet and sauté until golden brown, turning once. Remove from heat. Transfer chicken to a plate and set aside.

For the sauce, in same skillet add shallots, mushrooms, and garlic. Cook for 2 to 3 minutes or until softened, stirring constantly. Add wine and cook for 1 minute or until liquid is reduced by about one third. Add stock, tomatoes, and artichokes. Stir to combine and bring to a boil. Add parsley, oregano, salt, and pepper. Stir to combine. Remove from heat and set aside.

For the roux, in a small sauce pan melt butter. Whisk in flour for 2 to 3 minutes or until mixture thickens.

Place skillet with sauce back on heat and bring to a boil. Pour roux into the boiling sauce and stir constantly until sauce thickens. Immediately add chicken back to the pan; reduce heat and simmer mixture for 1 to 2 minutes or until chicken is heated through. Remove from heat.

To serve, equally divide pasta onto 4 individual dinner plates. Top with chicken and ladle sauce over top to cover. Serve immediately. Makes 4 servings.

Almond-Crusted Cod with Roasted Sweet Potatoes

This recipe could be your new favorite as it covers all the bases. It's light, healthy, beautiful and tasty!

POTATOES
10 large sweet potatoes, scrubbed, diced into 1-inch pieces, peel on
4 tablespoons olive oil
Salt and freshly ground black pepper to taste

FISH
4 ounces almonds, sliced, coarsely chopped
2 tablespoons dill, fresh, washed, finely chopped
3 lemons, washed, freshly zested
2 tablespoons extra virgin olive oil
¾ teaspoon kosher salt
¼ teaspoon coarsely ground black pepper
10 (4-ounce) portions of cod fish
2 tablespoons Dijon mustard

For the potatoes, preheat oven to 375 degrees. On a large rimmed baking sheet add potatoes, oil, salt, and pepper. Using your hands, gently toss to coat potatoes well. Place in oven and roast for 30 to 40 minutes or until potatoes turn light brown and easily pierced with a fork, turning once during cooking. Remove from oven and set aside in a warm place.

For the fish, in a small bowl add almonds, dill, oil, zest, salt, and pepper. Stir to combine and set aside. In a large baking dish add cod in a single layer. Using a pastry brush, lightly coat each piece of fish with the mustard, evenly dividing. Sprinkle the nut mixture over top of mustard, dividing evenly. Place in oven and bake, uncovered, for 10 to 12 minutes or until fish is opaque and flakes easily when tested with a fork. Remove from oven and set aside. Serve warm with the roasted rotatoes. Makes 10 servings.

Etc.

For a delicious light supper, pair this dish with warm, sautéed spinach or other seasonal greens on the side.

Beer Braised Brisket

Our own "BBQ Dude" Larry Hadley is known for his brisket. We strong-armed Larry (not really but we did have to bribe him!) to give us one of his recipes. This is one that we use often to make sandwiches on freshly baked focaccia bread. It's good stuff.

2 large carrots, peeled, chopped
1 onion, peeled, chopped
2 stalks celery, washed, chopped
3 tablespoons turbinado sugar
2 tablespoons Kosher salt
2 tablespoons fresh coarsely ground black pepper
1 tablespoon granulated garlic
1 medium size beef brisket, flat
3 sprigs thyme, fresh, washed
2 bottles wheat beer (we use our hometown brewer's version - Boulevard Brewing Company Unfiltered Wheat Beer)

Preheat oven to 350 degrees. In a baking dish add carrots, onion, and celery. Spread out across bottom of pan. In a small bowl add sugar, salt, pepper, and garlic. Stir to combine. Rub spice mix on all sides of brisket. Place brisket on top of vegetables in pan, fat side up. Top with the thyme sprigs. Pour beer into the bottom of pan and cover tightly with a plastic wrap and then a sheet of aluminum foil creating a good seal around the edges to keep liquid from escaping. Place in oven and bake for 3 to 4 hours or until instant-read thermometer reaches 185 to 195 degrees, depending on desired tenderness. Remove from oven and transfer brisket to a cutting board to allow it to rest for at least 10-15 minutes before slicing. Discard vegetables. Using a large sharp knife, cut brisket into slices and place on a serving platter. (Brisket may be cooked ahead, sliced and re-heated when ready to serve.) You may use the pan drippings to make a delicious sauce or gravy to pour over brisket slices when served. Serve warm. Serves 15 to 20.

Etc.

Many people are intimidated at the thought of making gravy from the drippings of their roasted meat, but it really couldn't be easier! First, strain the drippings through a sieve or cheesecloth into a glass measuring cup. Skim the fat off of the top of the drippings and transfer the drippings to a skillet or saucepan. (You need at least 3 tablespoons. If necessary, you may add a little melted butter to reach this amount.) Warm over medium-high heat, stirring occasionally. In a small bowl combine 2 to 3 tablespoons flour (or cornstarch) and 1 to 2 cups water. Whisk briskly to combine, then add to the skillet, stirring constantly. Cook and stir for 2 minutes or until gravy thickens. Season with salt and pepper. Remove from heat and pour into a gravy boat. Serve warm.

Chicken Spiedini with Amogia Sauce

This is the dish that my son in college asks for when he comes home. Time tested and "Devin approved!" Works for me!

AMOGIA SAUCE
2 lemons, freshly juiced
1 orange, freshly juiced
2 cloves garlic, peeled
1 shallot
½ cup mint, fresh
1 cup basil, fresh
Salt and freshly ground pepper to taste
1 cup extra virgin olive oil

CHICKEN
1 cup Italian breadcrumbs
¼ cup parmesan cheese, grated
2 (5- to 6-ounce) chicken breasts, skinless, boneless
1 slice prosciutto ham, divided
4 wooden skewers, soaked in water for 30 minutes
    (or metal skewers)
Oil, for grill

For the Amogia sauce, in a blender cup add juices, garlic, shallot, mint, basil, salt, and pepper. Puree for 20 seconds. With motor running, add oil in a thin stream and blend until combined. Set aside.

For the chicken, in a shallow dish add breadcrumbs and cheese. Stir to combine. Set aside. On a clean cutting board lay chicken breast and cover with a sheet of plastic wrap. Using the flat, smooth side of a tenderizing mallet, pound chicken breasts to about ¼-inch thick. Dredge each breast in the breadcrumb mixture and lay back on cutting board. Top each piece with 1 tablespoon Amogia sauce and ½-slice of ham. Using hands, roll up breasts away from you. Lay one roll in back of the other, butted up together. Insert four skewers evenly apart through rolls. Using a sharp knife, slice between each skewer. Dredge each piece in breadcrumbs again.

Preheat a charcoal or gas grill to medium-high heat and oil grates. Place skewers on grill and cook for 2 to 3 minutes per side or until instant-read thermometer reads 165 degrees. Remove from heat and transfer to individual dinner plates. Top with remaining sauce. Serve immediately. Makes 4 servings.

Etc.

Prosciutto is Italian for ham and usually refers to a thinly sliced, dry-cured ham. The most famous prosciutto comes from central and north Italy regions.

Cowboy KC Strip Steak with Tobacco Onions

STEAKS
2 tablespoons Ancho chili powder
1 tablespoon paprika
1 tablespoon kosher salt
2 teaspoons coarsely ground black pepper
1 tablespoon granulated garlic (or powder)
1 tablespoon sugar
4 tablespoons canola oil plus more for grates
4 (8- to 9-ounce) Kansas City strip steaks

ONIONS
1 large onion, peeled, cut into 1/8-inch slices
1/4 cup buttermilk
2 cups all-purpose flour
1 teaspoon salt
1 teaspoon granulated garlic
2 tablespoons chili powder

1/2 cup blue cheese, crumbled, for garnish

For steaks, preheat oven to 350 degrees. In a bowl combine chili powder, paprika, salt, pepper, garlic and sugar. Rub both sides of each steak with 2 tablespoons oil and a generous portion of seasoning. Heat grill to high and oil grates. Place steaks on grill and sear on each side for 2 minutes, turning twice, to achieve a temperature of medium rare. Adjust grilling time for desired doneness. Remove from grill to a baking sheet. Place in oven to finish to desired doneness. (3 to 5 minutes for medium as a guide). Remove from oven and transfer to a plate to rest.

For onions, preheat deep-fryer to 350 degrees. In a bowl add onions and buttermilk; toss to combine. In another small bowl add flour, salt, garlic and chili powder; toss to combine. Transfer onions to seasoning bowl. Toss gently to coat evenly. In deep fryer add onion slices, a handle full at a time. Fry for 30 seconds to 1 minute or until golden brown. Using a large slotted spoon (or tongs), remove from oil and transfer to a paper towel to drain. Repeat process with remaining onion slices.

To serve, place steaks on individual dinner plates. Top with onions, dividing evenly. Sprinkle with blue cheese, for garnish. Serve immediately. Makes 4 servings.

Etc.

Searing your steaks over high temperatures adds great flavor while keeping the juices inside! Use an instant read thermometer to ensure you are achieving the desired doneness of the meat. If you feel that the steak is too brown, and the thermometer is indicating rarer than you desire, move the steak to a cooler part of the grill to let it finish cooking.

Grilled Lamb with Rosemary

Once every summer, I make this dish for guests at my little cabin by the lake. I start with organic, grass-fed lamb purchased from a local farmer in northern Missouri. Even the folks who say they "don't eat lamb" can't resist this amazing dish!

MARINADE
½ cup raspberry vinegar (or red wine vinegar)
½ cup dry red wine
¼ cup soy sauce
¼ cup rosemary, fresh, washed, chopped
2 cloves garlic, fresh, peeled, chopped
1 teaspoon salt
1 teaspoon freshly ground black pepper

1 (3-pound) leg of lamb roast, boneless, rolled, tied
Oil, for grill

For the marinade, in a large re-sealable plastic bag add vinegar, wine, soy sauce, rosemary, garlic, salt, and pepper. Close bag tightly and gently shake to combine. Add lamb roast and gently shake until thoroughly covered with marinade. Place in refrigerator to marinate for 4 to 6 hours, turning occasionally.

When ready to cook, preheat gas grill to medium-high heat and lightly oil grates. Remove roast from refrigerator. In a large colander set over a bowl, transfer roast to drain, including marinade. Set marinade aside. Place roast on grill and cook for 15 minutes covered, turning once. Remove from the grill and place on a clean, flat surface. Wrap tightly in a sheet of aluminum foil and return to the grill. Close grill cover and cook for 30 minutes or until lamb reaches 135 to 140 degrees on an instant-read thermometer inserted into middle of the roast. (It will continue to cook as it rests.) Remove from grill and set aside on a cutting board, lightly covered with aluminum foil, for 10 minutes before carving. While lamb rests, in a small saucepan add reserved marinade. Bring liquid to a boil over medium-high heat for at least 1 minute or until heated through. Remove from heat and transfer to a serving bowl. Set aside.

To serve, using a large, sharp carving knife, slice roast. Transfer to serving platter. Serve warm with the sauce on the side. Makes 6 servings.

Etc.

Add a small bowl of prepared mint jelly to your table and let your guests add it to this amazing dish as desired.

Doris Laiben's Ultimate Eggplant Parmesan Casserole

The eggplant for this dish is baked instead of fried making it a lower fat, yet still flavorful, dish. Makes a great vegetarian alternative, although I am of the opinion that this dish pleases even the most dedicated carnivore too!

SAUCE
¼ *cup extra virgin olive oil*
1 large yellow onion, peeled, diced
4 cloves garlic, fresh, peeled, thinly sliced
3 tablespoons thyme leaves, fresh, washed, chopped
½ *medium carrot, peeled, finely grated*
2 (28-ounce) cans whole tomatoes, peeled,
    crushed by hand, juice reserved
Salt and freshly ground black pepper to taste

EGGPLANT
Spray oil, for pan
3 large eggplants, washed, sliced into
    1- to 1½-inch thick round slices
2 tablespoons extra virgin olive oil
Salt and freshly ground black pepper to taste

1 bunch basil leaves, fresh, washed, sliced, divided
1 pound mozzarella cheese, fresh,
    cut into ⅛*-inch slices, divided*
½ *cup parmesan cheese, plus more to taste,*
    freshly grated
¼ *cup breadcrumbs, fresh, lightly toasted*
    (preferably homemade)

For the sauce, in a large skillet heat oil over medium heat. Add onion and cook for 1 to 2 minutes or until softened, stirring constantly to prevent burning. Add garlic and cook for 1 to 2 more minutes or until onions and garlic turn golden brown, stirring constantly. Add thyme and carrots.

Etc.

Although the most popular variety is the dark purple color, eggplants can also be light green, yellow and a reddish color. You can usually substitute for what is in season or available at your local market. Eggplants are very perishable so it's best to purchase the same day (or day before) you plan to use them.

Cook for 5 minutes, stirring frequently. Add tomatoes, reserved tomato juice, salt, and pepper. Bring sauce to a boil, stirring frequently. Reduce heat to low and simmer for 30 minutes or until sauce thickens, stirring occasionally. Taste and adjust seasonings, if necessary. Remove from heat and set aside.

For the eggplant, preheat oven to 450 degrees. Lightly spray oil onto a large, rimmed baking sheet. Place as many eggplant slices as will fit onto pan. (You will need to bake the eggplant slices in batches.) Drizzle tops with oil and season with salt and pepper. Place in oven and bake for 15 minutes or until golden brown. Remove from oven and transfer slices to a plate (or wire rack) to cool. Repeat this process until all eggplant slices are baked.

To assemble, reduce oven temperature to 350 degrees. In a large, deep baking pan add largest slices of eggplant to cover bottom of the pan. Pour one-half of the sauce on top. Using the back of a large spoon (or a spatula) spread sauce evenly over layer of eggplant. Sprinkle one-half of the basil over top of sauce. Place 1 slice of mozzarella on top of each eggplant slice. Sprinkle one-third of the parmesan over entire casserole. Add second layer by repeating this process with the remaining eggplant slices, basil, mozzarella, and parmesan cheeses. Sprinkle breadcrumbs over the top of casserole. Place in the oven and bake for 20 minutes or until breadcrumbs are golden and cheese is melted. Remove from oven and set aside for about 10 minutes to cool. Serve hot. Makes 6 servings.

Grilled Salmon with Fresh Corn and Tomato Sauté

Thanks to Chef Gary Hild we have a beautiful healthful salmon recipe to share with you.

SAUTÉ
1 tablespoon olive oil
2 cloves garlic, peeled, smashed, finely minced
½ cup tomato, fresh, seeded, diced
½ cup corn (preferably fresh, cut off the cob, cooked)
1 tablespoon red wine vinegar
¼ cup heavy cream
2 tablespoons cilantro, fresh, washed, chopped
Kosher salt and freshly ground pepper to taste

SALMON
Oil, for grill
2 (5-ounce) salmon filets, skin on
2 tablespoons extra virgin olive oil
Kosher salt and freshly ground black pepper to taste

For the sauté, in a sauté pan heat oil over medium heat. Add garlic and sauté 1 minute or until brown and fragrant, stirring constantly making sure garlic doesn't burn. Add tomatoes and corn. Sauté for 1 minute, stirring frequently. Add vinegar and cook for a few seconds, stirring constantly. Add cream and continue to cook until sauce is reduced enough to coat all vegetables and has a creamy texture, stirring constantly. Remove from heat. Add cilantro, salt, and pepper. Stir to combine and set aside in a warm place.

For the salmon, clean grill grates and brush with oil. Preheat grill to high heat. Using a pastry brush, lightly brush the salmon with oil, evenly dividing. Season with salt and pepper. Place on grill, skin side up and cook for 1 minute; then turn ¼ turn on same side to create crosshatch marks. Continue to cook for 1 minute. Turn filets to skin side down and cook 2 minutes or until instant-read thermometer reaches 140 degrees. Remove from grill and place on a clean flat surface. Using a sharp paring knife, carefully remove skin from salmon and transfer to individual dinner plates. Top each with ¼ cup of the warm sauté. Serve immediately. Makes 2 servings.

Etc.

This entrée pairs well with fresh asparagus, your favorite green salad, and fresh avocado.

Leek & Tomato Quiche

A cookbook isn't complete without a great quiche recipe. Here is one of Chef Gary Hild's favorites.

CUSTARD
1-½ cups heavy cream
3 large eggs
3-½ ounces Monterey cheese, freshly grated
   (or Gruyere or cheddar)
1 tablespoon tarragon, fresh, washed, minced
1 tablespoon basil, fresh, washed, minced

FILLING
3 tablespoons butter
1 bunch scallions, peeled, white only, sliced thin
1-½ cups leeks, white and light green parts, sliced thin
1-½ cups tomato concassé, small dice
   (See note this page)
Salt and cayenne pepper to taste

1 (9-inch) pastry crust, partially baked

Preheat oven to 350 degrees.

For the custard, in a bowl add cream and eggs. Whisk until combined. Add cheese, tarragon, and basil. Using a large wooden spoon, gently stir to combine. Set aside.

For the filling, in a skillet heat butter over medium heat. Add scallions and leeks and sauté for 3 to 4 minutes or until translucent. Add the tomatoes and sauté until the liquid evaporates. Season with salt and cayenne. Remove from heat and set aside.

To assemble, gently spoon the filling into the prepared pie crust and spread out to cover bottom of the crust. Gradually pour the custard mixture into the filling. Using a fork, gently stir to distribute the filling ingredients evenly. Set the quiche inside a large baking dish filled with water about halfway up the side of the quiche pan. Place in the oven and bake for 40 to 45 minutes or until a sharp knife comes out clean when inserted in the center of the quiche. Remove from oven and set aside to cool. Serve warm or at room temperature. Makes 8 appetizer (or 6 entrée) servings.

Etc.

Concassé is a French cooking term, meaning to rough chop an ingredient, usually a vegetable. Tomato concassé is a process whereby the tomato is peeled, seeded and rough chopped or diced according to specific recipe instructions.

Mom's Holiday Brisket

I can't remember a Christmas Eve that Mom didn't serve this brisket on her dining room table. It was a kaleidoscope of holiday dishware, napkins and candles amidst dollar rolls, sliced cheese, coleslaw, potato salad and jars of homemade Christmas cookies. Sitting down to this meal always meant that opening presents was next.

SAUCE
½ cup chili sauce (such as Heinz)
1 cup bottled bbq sauce
   (preferably Original KC Masterpiece)
¼ cup brown sugar, packed
1 teaspoon onion salt
1 teaspoon garlic salt
½ cup prepared ketchup
1 tablespoon prepared mustard
½ to 1 cup water, divided

BRISKET
1 large beef brisket
1 to 2 tablespoons "Liquid Smoke" brand
   smoke flavoring

For the sauce, in a bowl add chili sauce, bbq sauce, brown sugar, onion salt, garlic salt, ketchup, mustard, and ½ cup water. Whisk to thoroughly combine, making sure that sugar is completely dissolved. (If sauce is too thick add remaining water.) Cover bowl with a sheet of plastic wrap and place in the refrigerator until ready to use.

For the brisket, preheat oven to 225 degrees. In a shallow baking pan add brisket. Using a pastry brush, lightly coat Liquid Smoke over all sides. Place in oven and cook for 7 hours or overnight. (Brisket will turn very dark when done, so don't worry.) Remove from oven and transfer brisket to a clean cutting board to cool. Raise the oven heat to 325 degrees. Using a large sharp knife, cut brisket into 1/8-inch slices. (It is important to cut slices against the grain of the beef.) Transfer slices by layering in an ovenproof casserole dish. Pour sauce over the top of meat. Tightly cover the pan with a sheet of aluminum foil (or casserole dish lid). Place in oven and bake for 30 minutes. Serve warm. Makes 12 to 18 servings.

Potato-Encrusted Tilapia Filets With Two Sauces

A very unusual recipe that has garnered many "oohs and aahs" at our private dinner parties. A great recipe to get your guests involved.

ARTICHOKE-TOMATO SAUCE
1 tablespoon butter, unsalted
1 large shallot, peeled, quartered
6 artichoke hearts, canned, cut into quarters, undrained
6 tomatoes, peeled, seeded, cut into wedges

CHAMPAGNE BUERRE BLANC SAUCE
½ cup champagne (or sparkling white wine)
2 tablespoons butter, unsalted, cut into ½-inch chunks
Salt and freshly ground black pepper to taste
1 tablespoon basil, fresh, washed, chiffonade

FISH
2 (5-ounce) Tilapia filets, fresh (or frozen, thawed)
Salt and freshly ground black pepper to taste
2 to 4 slices prosciutto, very thinly sliced, divided
2 to 3 cups grated potatoes, fresh, divided
¼ cup vegetable oil (or olive oil)

Etc.

Champagne is a specific form of sparkling wine that is produced in the region of Champagne in France. Champagne is produced following strict AOC production guidelines only found in this particular geographic region. All other sparkling wines are designated as simply 'sparkling wines.'

For the artichoke-tomato sauce, preheat a medium sauté pan over medium-high heat until very hot. Add butter and melt. Add shallots and sauté until slightly caramelized, stirring constantly to break shallots into pieces, being careful not to burn. Add the artichokes and tomatoes. Saute for 30 seconds. Remove from heat and transfer sauce to a bowl. Set aside and keep warm.

For the champagne buerre blanc sauce, in the same sauté pan over high heat add champagne. Cook until champagne is reduced by about a third, stirring and scraping the bottom of the pan. Add butter and melt, stirring constantly. Remove from heat and set aside. Add salt, pepper, and basil. Stir to combine well. Set aside and keep warm.

For the fish, preheat oven to 375 degrees. Place fish filets on a clean, flat surface and season with salt and pepper. Wrap a prosciutto slices completely around each filet. Using hands, pack grated potatoes around and on top of prosciutto and fish. Set aside. In a large ovenproof skillet heat oil over medium-high heat. Carefully lay potato wrapped fish into the oil. Cook for 2 to 3 minutes or until brown. Remove from heat. With a large spatula, carefully turn filets over in the pan. Place pan in oven and bake for 15 to 18 minutes or until temperature reads 135 degrees when instant-read thermometer is inserted into the center of fish. Remove from oven and set aside.

To serve, place 1 fish filet in center of an individual serving plate. Pour warmed artichoke-tomato sauce around fish and spoon warmed champagne sauce over top of fish. Serve immediately. Makes 2 servings.

Pork Rack with Apricot Cognac Sauce

Don't be nervous about preparing a full pork rack. This recipe will take you through each step. Brining is a very important part of this dish so don't leave it out.

PORK
¼ cup sea salt
1 gallon water plus more to cover meat, if needed
1 (8- to 10-bone) pork rack, Frenched
   (see note this page)
2 tablespoons kosher salt
1 tablespoon coarsely ground black pepper
2 tablespoons garlic, fresh, chopped

SAUCE
12 ounces apricot preserves
1 large red onion, peeled, chopped
2 cups water
⅔ cup apple cider vinegar
⅔ cup golden brown sugar, packed
¾ cup dried cherries, tart
¼ cup golden raisins
3 large cloves garlic, fresh, peeled, minced
2 teaspoons lemon zest, freshly grated
½ teaspoon salt
⅛ teaspoon cayenne pepper
½ cup Cognac liqueur

In a dutch oven or other deep stock pot add sea salt and water. Stir to combine. Place pork rack into water, making sure that pork is completely covered. Cover with a sheet of aluminum foil and place in the refrigerator overnight. When ready to roast, remove from refrigerator and remove pork from brine. Discard brine.

Preheat oven to 350 degrees. In a large sauté skillet add pork rack and sear for 1 to 2 minutes per side over high heat. Remove from heat and transfer to a roasting rack inside a baking dish. (Fit pan with a rack to elevate the pork.) Season all sides of pork with kosher salt, pepper, and garlic.

Place in oven and roast for 45 to 60 minutes or until internal temperature reaches 135 to 140 degrees when inserted with an instant-read thermometer. While pork is roasting making the apricot sauce below. Remove pork from oven and transfer to a large serving platter. Cover loosely with a sheet of aluminum foil and set aside to rest for 30 minutes. Using a large sharp knife, slice the pork rack between the chop bones. Serve warm with apricot sauce on the side, for garnish.

For the sauce, in a large saucepan add preserves, onion, water, vinegar, brown sugar, cherries, raisins, garlic, zest, salt, and cayenne pepper. Place on stove over medium-high heat and bring to a boil, stirring constantly until all sugar dissolves. Reduce heat to medium-low and simmer until all liquid has evaporated and sauce is thick, stirring occasionally. Remove from heat. Stir in cognac and set aside to cool. Transfer sauce to a blender and blend until smooth. Makes approximately 4 cups.

Tuscan-Style Strip Steaks

Hands down my favorite way to prepare steaks. I feel transported to the Tuscan countryside every time I make this dish!

HERB MIX
2 tablespoons basil, fresh, washed
2 tablespoons Italian parsley, fresh, washed
1 tablespoon rosemary, fresh, washed
¼ cup olive oil
1 tablespoon garlic, fresh, peeled, minced
1 anchovy
Sea salt to taste

STEAK
2 tablespoons olive oil plus more for grill
4 (12-ounce) strip steaks

DRESSING
¼ cup extra virgin olive oil
1 tablespoon aged balsamic vinegar
Sea salt and freshly ground black pepper to taste

4 cups arugula greens, washed, dried, divided

Parmigiano-Reggiano cheese, for garnish
4 lemon wedges, for garnish

For the herbs, in a food processor (or blender) add basil, parsley, rosemary, oil, garlic, and anchovy. Process by pulsing until thoroughly combined, but not pureed. Taste and season with salt. Set aside.

For the steaks, preheat gas grill (or cast-iron grill pan) over high heat and oil grates. With a pastry brush, coat 1/2 tablespoon of oil on each side of steaks. Place on grill and cook, turning once, until instant-read thermometer reaches 125 degrees (medium rare) when inserted into the thickest part of steaks. Remove from heat and set aside on a platter. Using hands, rub ½ tablespoon of herb mix on all sides of cooked steaks. Cover platter with a sheet of aluminum foil and set aside to allow the steaks to rest and the herbs to "marry" with the steak for 15 minutes.

To serve, in a small bowl add oil, vinegar, salt, pepper, and any steak juices that accumulated on platter. Whisk to combine and set aside. Evenly divide arugula and arrange on 4 individual dinner plates. Place 1 steak on top of greens and drizzle with dressing, evenly dividing. Using a vegetable peeler, shave Parmigiano-Reggiano cheese into long curls on top of steaks, for garnish. Add 1 lemon wedge on the side, for garnish. Serve warm. Makes 4 servings.

Shrimp in Garlic Cream with Mushrooms and Penne Pasta

An elegant dish that would be perfect for entertaining. Pair it with the same wine you used to cook it with.

¼ cup olive oil
25 (16-20 count per pound) shrimp, fresh, deveined, tails removed
1 pound button mushrooms, cleaned, sliced
1 tablespoon garlic, fresh, chopped
½ cup dry white wine, good quality (such as Pinot Grigio or Chardonnay)
1 cup heavy cream
2 cups penne pasta, cooked
Salt and freshly ground black pepper to taste
⅔ cup parmesan cheese, freshly grated

½ cup green onions, peeled, sliced, for garnish

In a large skillet heat oil over medium heat, add shrimp, mushrooms, and garlic. Sauté until shrimp are opaque and tails are curled. Remove from heat and transfer shrimp mixture to a bowl. Set aside. In the same skillet add wine and cook until reduced by one-half, stirring frequently. Add cream, bring to simmer and cook until the sauce is creamy and smooth, stirring frequently. Add the shrimp mixture and pasta. Gently stir to combine. Season with salt and pepper. Remove from heat. Portion pasta mixture into individual serving bowls. Sprinkle with the cheese, evenly dividing. Top with green onions, for garnish. Serve immediately. Makes 4 servings.

Etc.

Here's a rule of thumb when choosing a pasta shape: a lighter sauce calls for a smaller pasta, a bigger shape for a chunkier sauce and a thick sauce would be paired with a thicker pasta.

Lesson Five

Pastas

Chocolate Pasta

Giacomo's Baked Pasta Dish

"Grown-Up" Mac 'n Cheese

Lemon-Pine Nut Tagliatelle

*Linguine with Red Onion Marmalade,
Pancetta and Shrimp*

*Nonna's Orzo Pasta with
Sun-Dried Tomatoes and Pesto*

Noodles with Thai-Vietnamese Peanut Sauce

Orechiette con Cime di Rapa "Little Ear" Pasta with Broccoli Rabe

*Pumpkin and Three Cheese Ravioli with
Sage Walnut Butter Sauce*

Spaghetti alla Norma

Chocolate Pasta

Breath. It's true. There is such a thing! Chocolate pasta is an unusual delicacy and can be quite expensive if purchased in a specialty market or gourmet grocery store. Why not try it at home for much less!

1 pound cocoa powder
Hot water
1 tablespoon bittersweet chocolate, melted
1 large egg, room temperature
¾ cup semolina flour plus more for
*   kneading and rolling*
2 tablespoons sugar
1 gallon water
1 teaspoon salt

In a small bowl add cocoa powder and enough hot water to make a paste. In a large electric mixing bowl fitted with a dough hook add cocoa paste, chocolate, 1 egg, flour, and 2 tablespoons sugar. Blend for 5 minutes or until well combined, scraping sides of bowl frequently. Remove dough from the mixer and transfer to a lightly floured flat surface. Using your hands that have been lightly coated with flour, knead the dough until smooth, adding a little flour if the dough is too sticky. Wrap the dough with a sheet of plastic wrap and place in the refrigerator for 1 hour. Remove from refrigerator, unwrap, and place back on the lightly floured surface. Using a rolling pin that has been lightly dusted with flour, roll the dough out into a 1/16-inch thick piece. Using a sharp knife, cut the dough into the width and length of desired pasta (such as linguini or fettuccini), being careful not to make the individual pasta strands too long as this will make them unmanageable. (If you own a pasta machine, follow manufacturer instructions on rolling and cutting the pasta.) Transfer the finished noodles to a pasta drying rack (or scatter them on a large baking sheet that has been dusted with flour. Set aside. In a large stock pot add water and salt and bring to a boil over medium-high heat. Carefully add noodles, in batches, and cook for 2 to 3 minutes or until "al dente". Using a large slotted spoon, skim the noodles out of the water and place in colander to drain well. Serve cold (or warm) with your favorite sauce. Makes 6 to 8 servings.

Etc.

Serve as a decadent cold dessert with a rich, hazelnut cream sauce or flavored liqueur topped with fresh whipped cream and berries. You're sure to impress your family or dinner guests. Who knows, you might even get a standing ovation!

Giacomo's Baked Pasta Dish

In 1999, I took a group on a culinary tour of the Tuscany region of Italy. Our guide, Giacomo, was a "walking history book" as well as a fabulous Italian cook. I got pretty talented at jotting down his verbally shared recipes on matchbooks, travel brochures and napkins. This one was written on a paper napkin from a little restaurant in the ancient town of San Gimignano. It is simple and brings to mind many great memories of my trip every time I prepare it.

3 to 4 large onions, peeled, thinly sliced
6 to 8 ripe tomatoes (or 10 to 12 Roma tomatoes), washed, thinly sliced
½ to ¾ cup parmesan cheese, grated
1-½ cups dried bread crumbs
1 tablespoons dried oregano
4 to 5 cloves garlic, peeled, minced
Salt and freshly ground black pepper to taste
½ to ¾ cup olive oil
12 ounces dry bucatini pasta (or pasta of your choice), cooked al dente, drained

Preheat oven to 350 degrees. In a baking dish layer onions; then layer tomatoes on top. In a small bowl add cheese, bread crumbs, oregano, garlic, salt, and pepper. Stir to combine. Sprinkle mixture over top of tomatoes, covering evenly. Drizzle oil on top. Transfer to oven and bake for about 20 minutes, checking often to make sure it does not dry out or burn. Remove from the oven. Remove from pan to a clean cutting board. Using a large, sharp knife, coarsely chop. Transfer to a large serving bowl. Add pasta and gently toss to combine. Serve cold, warm or hot. Makes 8 servings.

Etc.

The better the quality of tomatoes, the tastier the finished product will be. You can also easily vary the amount of ingredients to suit your taste buds.

"Grown-Up" Mac 'n Cheese

This decadent version of the classic macaroni and cheese has become a constant in our Dinners on Demand™ program which offers frozen chef-prepared dishes for sale. For heaven's sake, it has bacon so how can you go wrong?

TOPPING
2 cups Panko bread crumbs
¼ cup butter, unsalted, melted

PASTA
1 gallon water
1 tablespooon salt
1 pound cavatappi pasta, dry

SAUCE
½ pound bacon, roughly cut into small pieces
1 onion, chopped
5 tablespoons butter, unsalted
6 tablespoons all purpose flour
1-½ teaspoons Dijon mustard
2 teaspoons roasted garlic pepper seasoning
¼ teaspoon cayenne pepper
    (or 2 tablespoons prepared hot sauce)
3 cups milk
2 cups chicken stock
4 ounces Monterrey Jack cheese, shredded
4 ounces sharp cheddar cheese, shredded
Salt and freshly ground black pepper, to taste

For the topping, in a bowl add bread crumbs and butter. Using a spoon, toss to combine well. Set aside.

For the pasta, in a medium stockpot, add the water and salt. Bring to boil over high heat. Add pasta and cook until pasta is tender. Remove from heat and drain in colander. Set aside.

For the sauce, in a heavy skillet, add bacon and brown on medium heat, stirring frequently. Using a slotted spoon remove bacon and set aside, leaving rendered fat in skillet. Add onions to bacon fat and cook until translucent. Using a slotted spoon remove onions and place in container with bacon. Set aside.

In same medium stockpot, add butter and melt over medium-high heat until foaming, stirring constantly. Add flour, mustard, garlic seasoning, and cayenne. Whisk for one minute or until mixture becomes fragrant and deepens in color. Gradually add milk and stock and whisk to combine. Bring mixture to a boil, whisking constantly (mixture must reach full boil to fully thicken.) Reduce heat to low and simmer for 5 minutes or until thickened to consistency of heavy cream, whisking occasionally. Remove from heat.

Add cheeses, salt and pepper. Whisk mixture until cheeses are fully melted and incorporated into the sauce. Add pasta and reserved bacon and onions and mix well. Transfer to an oven-safe baking dish. Preheat oven to 350 degrees. Bake for approximately 30 minutes or until cheese is bubbly. Remove from oven and top evenly with prepared topping. Turn oven settings to broil and broil for 3 to 5 minutes or until topping is a deep golden brown, rotating pan for even browning, if necessary. Remove from oven and set aside for 5-10 minutes to cool slightly. Serve warm. Makes 4 to 6 servings.

Lemon-Pine Nut Tagliatelle

I came across this dish in the little town of San Gimingano, Italy when I took a group there in 1999 on a culinary tour. We were treated to lunch on the sun porch of an olive oil estate. You could hear a pin drop as the group was eating this dish. It's really that special...and even more elegant when made with fresh pasta.

SAUCE
½ cup pines nuts
1 cup flat-leaf parsley, fresh, washed, minced, gently packed
½ cup extra virgin olive oil
2 lemons, freshly zested
Fine sea salt and freshly ground black pepper to taste

PASTA
1 gallon water
1 teaspoon salt
1-½ pounds tagliatelle (fettuccini), preferably freshly made and slightly dried

Salt and freshly ground black pepper to taste
1 lemon, fresh, washed, cut into 6 wedges, for garnish

For the sauce, preheat oven to 300 degrees. On a large rimmed baking sheet add pine nuts. Place in oven for 3 to 5 minutes or until lightly toasted. Remove from oven and transfer to a small bowl. Add parsley, oil, lemon zest, salt, and pepper. Stir until well combined. Cover bowl with a sheet of plastic wrap and set aside for at least 2 hours at room temperature.

For the pasta, in a large stock pot add water and salt. Bring to a boil over medium-high heat. Add tagliatelle and cook according to package directions. Remove from heat and drain through a colander, reserving ½ cup of the cooking water.

To serve, in a large serving bowl add hot pasta, reserved cooking water, and prepared sauce. Using large tongs, gently toss until well combined. Season with salt and pepper. Serve warm with lemon wedges on the side, for garnish. Makes 6 servings

Linguine with Red Onion Marmalade, Pancetta and Shrimp

Chef Jason Street taught with us in the early years of The Culinary Center and his nick-name was "King of Flavor!" In addition to being a wonderful sauce for pasta, this recipe also makes an excellent topping for crostini or bruschetta appetizers.

MARMALADE
3 medium red onions, peeled, julienned
1 cup burgundy wine (or other red wine)
1 cup balsamic vinegar
1 cup brown sugar, packed
1 teaspoon garlic, minced
1 teaspoon freshly cracked black pepper
6 tablespoons olive oil

PASTA
1 to 2 tablespoons olive oil
4 ounces pancetta, very finely diced
2 to 3 cloves garlic, peeled, minced
1 tablespoon crushed red pepper flakes
1-½ cups dry white wine
1 pound medium rock shrimp, fresh, shelled, deveined
½ cup Red Onion Marmalade
Salt and freshly ground black pepper to taste
12 ounces dry linguine, cooked, drained
¼ cup butter, unsalted, room temperature
¼ cup parsley, fresh, washed, chopped

For the marmalade, in a medium saucepan add onions, wine, vinegar, brown sugar, garlic, pepper, and oil. Stir to combine. Cover with lid and cook over medium heat for 30 minutes or until liquid is reduced by half, stirring occasionally. Set aside.

For the pasta, in a large sauté pan heat oil over medium heat. Add pancetta and sauté for 10 minutes or until it becomes translucent. Add garlic, pepper flakes, wine, shrimp, and marmalade. Bring to a boil, stirring occasionally to prevent marmalade from burning. Season with salt and pepper. Add pasta, butter and parsley. Gently toss to combine. Transfer pasta to a large, warm serving bowl. Serve warm. Makes 4 to 5 servings.

Etc.

Pancetta is an un-smoked Italian bacon that is cured with salt and spices. It can be found in the deli section of most major grocery stores as well as at specialty Italian markets. Bacon may be substituted, if desired.

Nonna's Orzo Pasta with Sun-Dried Tomatoes and Pesto

Serve this colorful dish warm or at room temperature. It makes a beautiful side dish or fan grilled chicken across the top of a mound and call it dinner. Use the best olive oil you have as the flavor will come through in this simple and hearty dish.

PESTO
3 tablespoons pine nuts
2 cups basil, fresh, washed
2 cloves garlic, fresh, whole
½ teaspoon salt
Dash of freshly ground black pepper
2/3 cup olive oil
¾ cup parmesan cheese, freshly grated

PASTA
1 gallon water
1 tablespoon salt
½ pound orzo pasta, dry
3 tablespoons extra virgin olive oil, divided
2 cloves garlic, fresh, peeled, chopped
½ cup sun-dried tomatoes, sliced
   (may be substituted with prepared in oil)
½ cup basil pesto
Kosher salt and freshly ground black pepper
   to taste

For the pesto, preheat oven to 325 degrees. On a large rimmed baking sheet arrange pine nuts in a single layer. Place in oven and roast until the nuts brown. (You'll know it's close when you can smell the pine nuts.) Remove from oven. In a food processor fitted with a steel blade add nuts, basil, garlic, salt, and pepper. Puree until well combined, scraping sides as needed. While motor is running add oil in a thin, steady stream and blend until emulsified. Turn off motor and add cheese. Pulse mixture briefly to incorporate cheese, being careful not to over-mix. Transfer pesto to a bowl and cover with a sheet of plastic wrap. Place in refrigerator for up to 1 day or until ready to use. (Pesto may also be kept in freezer for several months.)

For the pasta, in a large stock pot add water and salt. Bring to a boil over medium-high heat. Add pasta and cook for 8 to 9 minutes or to "al dente." Remove from heat and drain in a colander. Immediately spray pasta with cold tap water to stop the cooking process. Drizzle 2 tablespoons of the oil over top of pasta. Using large tongs, gently toss to coat well. Set aside. In a saucepan heat remaining 1 tablespoon olive oil over medium heat. Add garlic and cook for 1 to 2 minutes or until it starts to turn golden brown, stirring constantly to prevent burning. Immediately add tomatoes and pasta to stop garlic from cooking further. Add pesto, salt, and pepper. Using large tongs, gently toss until well combined. Transfer to a large serving bowl. Serve warm. Makes 4 servings.

Noodles with Thai-Vietnamese Peanut Sauce

What would a collection of pasta recipes be without including one for Asian noodles? This recipe is very versatile and can be served at almost any temperature. A quick trip to an Asian market and you will have all of the ingredients necessary for this fabulous, tasty dish.

SAUCE
½ cup coconut milk
2 tablespoons red curry paste
½ cup peanut butter, creamy
½ cup water
3 tablespoons brown sugar
1 lime, freshly juiced
1 tablespoon Asian fish sauce
½ teaspoon salt

1 pound dry Asian egg noodles
    (or thin spaghetti), cooked, drained

Broccoli, fresh, chopped, steamed, for topping
Peanuts, chopped, for topping
Cilantro, washed, chopped, for topping
Scallions, washed, peeled, chopped, for topping

For the sauce, in a saucepan add milk, paste, peanut butter, water, brown sugar, juice, fish sauce, and salt. Stir to combine. Place on stove and bring to a boil over medium-high heat, whisking constantly until smooth. Remove from heat and set aside to cool to room temperature.

In a large serving bowl add noodles. Pour sauce over top and gently toss to combine. Transfer equal portions to individual dinner plates and serve with toppings of your choice. Serve warm. Makes 6 to 8 servings.

Orechiette con Cime di Rapa
("Little Ear" Pasta with Broccoli Rabe)

This is a great dish to showcase the healthy ingredient of broccoli rabe!

3 quarts water
1 teaspoon salt
1 pound dry orechiette pasta
*   (or small shell pasta or ziti)*
1 to 2 bunches broccoli rabe,
*   washed, trimmed*
¼ extra virgin olive oil
4 cloves garlic, fresh, peeled,
*   crushed (or chopped)*
Pinch of crushed red pepper flakes
¼ cup parmesan cheese (or Romano),
*   freshly grated*

In a large pot add water and salt. Bring to a boil. Add pasta and cover pot. When water returns to a boil, add broccoli rabe. Continue to boil until pasta is cooked al dente. (The pasta will be infused with the flavor of the greens.) Before draining the pasta and greens, ladle out 2 cups of the liquid into a bowl to reserve. Remove pot and drain the pasta and greens in a colander. Set aside. In a skillet heat oil over medium-high heat. Add garlic and crushed red pepper and sauté until the garlic is browned, stirring constantly to prevent burning. To serve, in a large pasta bowl add pasta and greens. Pour garlic and crushed peppers over top and gently toss to combine, adding some of the reserved cooking liquid, if needed. Top with cheese. Serve warm. Makes 6 to 8 servings.

Etc.

Broccoli rabe (also called "brocoletti de rape", "rape" or "rapini") has a pungent, butter flavor that is popular in Italian cooking. To clean broccoli rabe, cut and discard the lower stems that are hard as well as some of the extra leaf-like foliage. The remainder should be roughly cut into bite-sized pieces. If you are a fan of anchovies, substitute four anchovy fillets for the parmesan cheese in this recipe.

Pumpkin and Three Cheese Ravioli with Sage Walnut Butter Sauce

This was a signature dish for us under the helm of our first Executive Chef Nancy Stark. Don't knock the pumpkin filling until you've tried it – it's heavenly! The simple sauce of butter with walnuts and sage is drizzled on sparingly to add a richness and fullness to the dish. We use this recipe when guests want to be involved in some "hands-on" dinner preparation. They love to see how easy it is to make your own stuffed ravioli.

SAUCE
½ cup butter, unsalted
⅓ cup walnuts, coarsely chopped
13 sage leaves, fresh, 8 cut fine chiffonade
*   plus 5 whole, for garnish*
Salt and freshly ground pepper to taste

RAVIOLI
1 tablespoon olive oil
¼ cup onion, finely chopped
2 cloves garlic, whole, minced
1-½ cups pumpkin, roasted, roughly pureed
1 cup ricotta cheese, crumbled
½ cup feta cheese, crumbled
½ cup parmesan cheese, freshly grated
3 large egg yolks, lightly beaten
Pinch of nutmeg
Pinch of cayenne
Salt and freshly ground black pepper to taste
40 wonton wrappers (available in produce
*   section of most grocery stores)*
1 large egg white, lightly beaten
Water, for cooking
1 teaspoon salt, for water

Etc.

Chiffonade is a cutting method that allows leafy vegetables and herbs to be formed into ribbons or thin strips, usually for garnishes. While basil is easily the most common herb used for this sort of knife technique, other herbs such as the fresh sage called for in this recipe also work well. Simply stack multiple leaves and roll them into a tight cylinder shape. Using a very sharp knife, cut the herb cylinder horizontally creating aromatic ribbons that release the herbs natural oils and create a more intense flavor. Leafy vegetables such as spinach, kale and cabbage may also be used for this technique. If you wish to make the chiffonade ahead of time, simply immerse the ribbons into a cool water bath to prevent discoloration.

For the sauce, in a heavy skillet melt butter. Continue to cook on low heat until golden brown and giving off a nutty aroma. Remove from heat. Add walnuts and sage chiffonades, salt, and pepper and gently stir to combine. Set aside.

For the ravioli, in a large sauté pan heat olive oil and sauté onions until soft and golden brown, stirring constantly to prevent burning. Remove from heat. Add garlic and pumpkin. Gently stir to combine well. Transfer mixture to a medium mixing bowl. Add ricotta, feta, and parmesan cheese. Stir well to combine. Very gradually add beaten egg yolks and gently stir to combine. (Filling should be moist but not runny.) Add nutmeg and cayenne, salt, and pepper. Stir to combine thoroughly.

To prepare, on a clean, flat surface place one wonton wrapper. Put one tablespoon of filling in the middle of wrapper. Using a pastry brush (or your fingers), brush the edges of wrapper with egg white and top with another wrapper. Press edges together lightly to seal. (Make sure there are no edges left unsealed or filling will leak during the cooking process.) Repeat this process until all filling is used. In a large saucepan add salt and enough water to fill ¾ of pan and bring to a boil over medium-high heat. Carefully drop the ravioli, one by one, into the boiling water. Cook for 3 minutes or until the ravioli floats to the surface. Using a large slotted spoon, remove ravioli from water and transfer to warm dinner plates. Top with sauce. Add one whole sage leaf to each plate, for garnish. Serve warm. Makes 4 to 5 servings.

Spaghetti alla Norma

Just like an Italian Grandmother would make. This pasta dish is made with eggplant, cheese, and tomato sauce. An Italian favorite!

EGGPLANT
1 large (or 2 small) eggplant, washed, ends removed, cut crosswise into ½-inch thick slices
Salt to taste
⅓ cup vegetable oil

SAUCE
⅓ cup olive oil
1 large yellow onion, peeled, finely chopped
2 cloves garlic, fresh, peeled, minced
2 to 2-½ pounds tomatoes, fresh, peeled, seeded, chopped
Salt and freshly ground black pepper to taste
1 cup basil leaves, fresh, washed, torn into pieces

PASTA
1 gallon water
1 teaspoon salt
1 pound spaghetti, dry

½ cup ricotta salata cheese, coarsely grated, plus extra, for garnish
½ cup parmesan cheese, freshly grated

For the eggplant, in a large colander add eggplant slices, in layers, sprinkling with salt after each layer. Place the colander over a bowl (or in sink). Place a plate on top of eggplant; then a heavy weight pot on top of the plate. Let stand for 1 hour to drain off the bitter juices of the eggplant. Remove pot and plate. Rinse the eggplant under cool water to remove salt and dry thoroughly with paper towels. Set aside. In a large skillet heat oil over medium heat. Add enough eggplant slices to make a single layer in skillet. (You will need to cook eggplant in batches.) Fry for 8 minutes or until tender and lightly browned, turning once. Transfer to a baking sheet covered in paper towels to drain. Using a sharp knife, cut the eggplant slices into one-inch strips. Set aside.

Etc.

The dish "Spaghetti all Norma" was first created in the city of Catania , the second largest city in Sicily. It was dedicated by a Catania composer who wrote the famous opera lirica "LA NORMA" in 1831.

For the sauce, in a large saucepan heat oil over medium heat. Add onions and cook for 5 minutes or until tender, stirring frequently to prevent burning. Add garlic and cook for 30 seconds, stirring constantly. Reduce heat to low. Add tomatoes, salt, and pepper. Simmer, uncovered, for 20 minutes or until just thickened. Add eggplant slices and basil. Gently stir to combine well and set aside.

In a large stock pot add water and salt. Bring to a boil over medium-high heat. Add spaghetti and cook until package directions or until "al dente". Remove from heat and drain through a colander. Transfer spaghetti back to pot. Add sauce, ½ cup ricotta salata cheese and parmesan cheese. Using large tongs, gently toss until pasta is well coated. Transfer to a large serving bowl. Top with ricotta salata cheese, for garnish. Serve immediately. Makes 6 servings.

Lesson Six

Vegetarian & Side Dishes

Baked Peppers with Ricotta and Basil

Barley & Wild Mushroom Risotto

Crispy 'Oven-Fried' Red Potatoes

Frijoles Charros ("Dressed Up" Beans)

Grilled Polenta Cakes

Pan-Roasted Corn With Chilies

Rice Pilaf With White Raisins, Cognac And Pistachios

Simply Elegant Potato Gratin With Gruyere

Wild Rice and Orzo with Toasted Walnuts and Dried Cranberries

Wild Mushroom Cheese Tart

Broccoli Soufflé

Baked Peppers with Ricotta and Basil

We adapted this recipe from the popular book "Under the Tuscan Sun" by Frances Mayes. Over the years we have found that any class with "Tuscan" in the title will fill quickly. I think it is because Tuscan cuisine focuses on simple ingredients and preparations but results in amazing dishes.

Oil, for grill
3 large yellow bell peppers, whole, washed
½ tablespoon olive oil
2 cups ricotta cheese
½ cup basil, fresh, washed, chopped
½ cup green onions, washed, peeled, thinly sliced
½ cup Italian parsley, fresh, washed, minced
Salt and freshly ground black pepper to taste
2 large eggs, lightly beaten
Basil leaves, fresh, washed, stems removed,
　　for garnish

Preheat oven to 350. Heat a gas grill to high heat and lightly oil grates. Place peppers on grill until charred all over, turning with tongs as needed and making sure you don't cook them so long that they turn limp. Remove from grill and place on a cutting board until cooled to the touch. Using a sharp knife, cut peppers in half and clean out ribs and seeds. Transfer to a baking sheet, skin side down so that peppers form a "bowl". Drizzle with oil and set aside. In a large bowl add cheese, basil, onions, parsley, salt, and pepper. Stir to combine. Add eggs and gently stir mixture to combine well. Stuff peppers with the cheese mixture, evenly dividing.

Place in oven and bake for 30 minutes or until peppers are heated through. Remove from oven. Top with basil leaves, for garnish. Serve warm. Makes 6 servings.

Barley & Wild Mushroom Risotto

A non–traditional take on classic risotto. This version is made with barley. You can educate your guests as well as feed them well. Imagine that!

2 cups dried porcini mushrooms
¼ cup olive oil, divided
2 cloves garlic, fresh, peeled, chopped
¼ cup parsley, fresh, finely chopped, divided
6 cups chicken stock
¼ cup butter, clarified
½ cups shallots, minced
1-½ cups barley (or farro) (See note this page)
½ cup white wine, dry
Salt and pepper to taste
4 tablespoons Parmesan Reggiano, grated

To rehydrate dried mushrooms, pour hot water over them and let "plump" for 1 hour. Drain off excess water and squeeze the mushrooms to purge any extra liquid.

For the mushrooms, in a skillet add 3 tablespoons oil and heat over medium heat. Add mushrooms and garlic. Sauté for 2 to 3 minutes. Add 2 tablespoons parsley and mix to combine. Set aside.

For the risotto, in a saucepan add broth and simmer. Meanwhile, in a different saucepan heat butter in remaining one tablespoon oil over medium heat. Add shallots and cook over moderate heat for 3 to 4 minutes or until soft and golden, stirring often. Add barley and cook for 4 to 6 minutes or until toasted, stirring constantly. Add wine and continue cooking until liquid evaporates. With a ladle, pour in one ladle of stock and cook until absorbed, stirring constantly. Turn heat to medium. Add another ladle of stock and cook until absorbed. Continue this process and cook for 20 to 25 minutes or until the barley is tender. Season with salt and pepper. Add mushroom mixture, remaining 2 tablespoons parsley and cheese. Stir to combine. Transfer to a serving bowl. Serve warm. Makes 8 servings.

Etc.

Barley and farro may be used interchangeably because of their similar characteristics. They are both hulled wheat typically used in salads, soups and side dishes.

Crispy 'Oven-Fried' Red Potatoes

The secret to these tasty potatoes is that you toss them in the aioli before baking. The egg and oil in the aioli makes the crisping part a snap.

16 small red potatoes, whole, scrubbed, dried, skin left on
Water, for cooking (enough to cover potatoes in pan by 2-inches)
3 to 4 tablespoons extra virgin olive oil
Kosher salt (or sea), coarsely ground, to taste
¼ cup aioli, thinned with 1 to 2 tablespoons water (see Aioli recipe in this cookbook under "Little Extras.")

Preheat oven to 475 degrees. In a large saucepan add potatoes and water. Cover and bring to a boil over medium-high heat. Reduce heat to medium and continue to cook, partially covered, for 20 minutes or until potatoes are completely tender when pierced by a fork. (Do not overcook.) Remove from heat. Using a colander, drain potatoes and set aside until cool to the touch. Transfer to a clean cutting board. Using a sharp knife, cut potatoes into quarters and transfer to a large mixing bowl. Add oil, salt and aioli. Using a large spoon, gently toss to until potatoes are coated, taking care not to crush potatoes. Transfer to a large, rimmed baking sheet and arrange potatoes in a single layer. Place in oven and bake for 45 minutes or until potatoes are crisp and golden brown, turning once in the middle of baking. Remove from oven and transfer to a large serving bowl. Serve warm. Makes 4 to 6 servings.

Frijoles Charros
("Dressed Up" Beans)

PICO de GALLO
6 Roma tomatoes, washed, medium dice
1 large onion, peeled, medium dice
1 jalapeno pepper, washed, seeded, minced
½ bunch cilantro, fresh, washed, chopped
½ lemon, freshly juiced
½ lime, freshly juiced
Salt and freshly ground black pepper to taste

BEANS
1 gallon water
2 tablespoons salt
2 cups dried pinto beans, rinsed
2 cups pico de gallo
1 cup chorizo sausage, cooked, chopped
½ pound bacon, cooked, drained, chopped
½ bottle beer

For the pico de gallo, in a bowl add tomatoes, onion, pepper, cilantro, lemon and lime juice, salt, and pepper. Stir together to combine. Set aside. (Remaining pico de gallo may be stored in refrigerator in an air-tight non-reactive container for up to two days.)

For the beans, in a large pot add water and salt and bring water to a boil. Reduce heat to simmer and add beans. Cook uncovered for 1-1/2 to 2 hours or until beans are tender and liquid is absorbed. Add pico de gallo, sausage, bacon, and beer. Using a large spoon, mix until ingredients are well combined being careful not to smash beans. Transfer to a large serving bowl. Serve warm. Makes approximately 4 cups.

Etc.

This tasty dish is a Mexican tradition. It was named in honor of Mexican charros (or horsemen) and is also known as "Cowboy Beans." The base of the dish is always pinto beans which are cooked with seasonings such as garlic, bacon, and hot peppers. A perfect addition to your backyard BBQ!

Grilled Polenta Cakes

Experience polenta in a whole new way!

2 tablespoons olive oil, plus extra for grilling
¾ cup red onion, finely chopped
2 cloves garlic, peeled, finely minced
1 quart chicken stock (or broth)
1 cup coarse ground cornmeal
3 tablespoons butter, unsalted
1-½ teaspoons kosher salt
¼ teaspoon freshly ground black pepper
2 ounces parmesan cheese, grated

Preheat the oven to 350 degrees. Line a 9" x 13" cake pan with parchment paper and set aside. In a large oven-safe saucepan heat oil over medium heat. Add onion and cook for 4 to 5 minutes or until they begin to turn translucent, stirring constantly. Reduce the heat to low. Add garlic and sauté for 1 to 2 minutes, stirring constantly to prevent burning. Turn heat back up to high. Add stock and bring to a boil. Gradually add the cornmeal, a little at a time, whisking to combine after each addition. Place in oven and cook for 35 to 40 minutes or until mixture is creamy, stirring every 10 minutes to prevent lumps from forming. Remove from oven. Add butter, salt, pepper, and cheese. Using a large spoon, stir mixture together until butter and cheese are melted and all ingredients are thoroughly combined. Pour polenta into the cake pan, cover and place in the refrigerator until completely cooled.

To serve, heat a gas grill (or non-stick sauté skillet) over medium heat. Remove polenta from the refrigerator and turn out onto a clean cutting board. Using a sharp knife, cut into square, round, or triangle shapes. Using a pastry brush (or spray oil), coat each side of the polenta cakes with oil. Place on the hot grill and cook until heated through and grill marks are evident. Remove from grill and transfer to a serving platter. Serve warm. Makes 8+ servings.

Pan-Roasted Corn With Chilies

What is it about using simple quality ingredients that marry beautifully that makes us crazy. This one is crazy good. Use fresh corn and go nuts.

¼ cup canola oil
4 cups sweet corn niblets, frozen
½ small onion, peeled, small dice
2 jalapeno peppers, washed, seeded, minced
1 teaspoon kosher salt
½ teaspoon freshly ground white pepper

In a large skillet heat oil over medium-high heat. Add corn, onions, and peppers. Cook for 5 minutes or until onions and peppers are soft, stirring frequently. Reduce heat to low and continue to cook for 5 to 10 minutes or until mixture is caramelized. Season with salt and pepper. Remove from heat and transfer to a serving bowl. Serve warm. Makes 4 cups.

Etc.

Caramelization is the browning of sugar, a cooking technique used to achieve nutty flavor and brown color.

Rice Pilaf with White Raisins, Cognac and Pistachios

Here's an interesting recipe for rice pilaf that will set you apart from other cooks. It is easy to prepare and the result is quite refined.

½ cup white raisins
¼ cup Cognac
6 tablespoons butter, unsalted
¼ cup shallots, peeled, chopped
½ teaspoon salt
1 cup long grain brown rice, cooked
1 cup wild rice, cooked
¼ cup pistachio nuts, chopped

Preheat oven to 250 degrees. In a small bowl add raisins and Cognac. Soak for 10 minutes. In a skillet melt butter. Add undrained raisins and Cognac. Saute for 5 minutes. Add shallots and continue to sauté for a few more minutes. Add salt, brown rice, wild rice, and nuts. Gently toss to combine. Transfer mixture to the baking dish and place in oven. Cook for 15 to 20 minutes. Serve warm. Makes 4 servings.

Etc.

For an elegant menu for entertaining, serve this dish with raspberry balsamic glazed cornish hens and glazed carrots.

Simply Elegant
Potato Gratin with Gruyere

Simple ingredients can make utterly elegant dishes. Enough said!

Spray oil, for pan
5 large baking potatoes, peeled,
    cut to ³⁄₈-inch slices
Coarse sea salt and freshly ground
    black pepper to taste
1 large clove garlic, fresh, peeled, finely minced
1-½ to 2 cups milk
1-½ cups Gruyere cheese, grated
    (or finely chopped)
¼ cup butter, unsalted

Preheat oven to 375 degrees and lightly spray a 9" x 13" baking dish. In a saucepan add potato slices and season well with salt and pepper. Add garlic and enough milk so that potatoes are ½ to ¾ covered. Simmer potatoes on the stovetop over medium heat for 20 minutes, stirring occasionally to prevent scorching. Transfer potato mixture to the prepared baking dish. Spread cheese evenly over the top and dot with butter. Place in oven and cook for 45 minutes to one hour or until sauce is thickened and potatoes are tender and nicely browned. Remove from oven. Serve warm. Makes 4 servings.

Wild Rice and Orzo with Toasted Walnuts and Dried Cranberries

This unique dish can be served on its own as a light vegetarian lunch (or perhaps with strips of grilled chicken fanned on top) or as a side dish. We like to mound it in a colorful round bowl and serve it on a buffet. It also makes a great picnic dish because it can be served at room temperature.

1-½ cups wild rice, cooked, well drained
6 tablespoons walnut oil (or extra virgin olive oil), divided
1 pound orzo, cooked 'al dente,' well drained
3 tablespoons lemon juice plus additional to taste, divided
Salt and freshly ground black pepper to taste
⅔ cup scallions, peeled, finely chopped
1 cup walnuts, toasted, chopped
1 cup dried cranberries

In a large bowl add rice and 2 tablespoons oil. Stir to combine. Add orzo and the remaining 4 tablespoons oil, juice, salt and pepper. Stir to combine. (Mixture may be prepared up to this step one day ahead, covered and chilled.)

Immediately before serving add scallions, walnuts, and cranberries. Gently stir to mix well. Transfer to a serving bowl and season with additional lemon juice. Serve at room temperature. Makes 10 to 12 servings.

Etc.

In Italian, orzo means barley but it is actually a tiny rice-shaped pasta that can be substituted for rice in most recipes.

Wild Mushroom Cheese Tart

A beautiful side dish, this recipe can also double as an appetizer or even a vegetarian entrée.

CRUST
1-¼ cups all-purpose flour plus more for rolling
½ teaspoon salt
½ cup butter, unsalted, chilled, cut into pieces
2 tablespoons ice water

FILLING
1 cup water
1 ounce porcini mushrooms, dried
¼ cup butter, unsalted
10 ounces shitake (or button) mushrooms,
*   cleaned, dried, sliced*
Salt to taste
¼ cup shallots, minced
2 tablespoons brandy
2 tablespoons thyme, fresh, washed, chopped, divided
⅓ cup white cheddar cheese, grated, divided

¾ cup whipping cream
1 large egg
2 large egg yolks

For the crust, in a food processor add flour and salt. Process until blended. Using the pulse button, cut butter in until mixture resembles coarse meal. Add enough water, 1 tablespoon at a time, to blend dough. Using your hands, form dough into a ball and wrap tightly in a sheet of plastic wrap. Place in refrigerator for at least 45 minutes. Remove from refrigerator and transfer to a lightly floured flat surface (or pastry cloth). Using a floured rolling pin, roll dough into a 12-inch round. Transfer to a 9-inch tart pan with a removable bottom. Using a sharp knife, trim overlapping dough leaving a 1/2-inch overhang. Using your fingers, fold overhang under to form double-thick edge all the way around the pan. Press tart edges up to raise dough 1/8-inch above pan. Place in refrigerator for 30 minutes to chill. Preheat oven to 350 degrees. Remove tart crust from refrigerator and line the edges with aluminum foil. Fill inside of pan with dried beans (or pie weights.) to prevent crust from rising. Place in oven and bake for 15 minutes. Remove from oven. Remove foil and discard beans. Place back in oven and continue to bake for 15 minutes or until golden. Remove from oven and set aside on a wire rack to cool.

For the filling, in a saucepan add water and bring to a boil. Add porcini mushrooms; remove from heat and let stand for 30 minutes. Using a spoon, remove mushrooms, reserving liquid, and coarsely chop. Place a double-thickness of cheesecloth (or a coffee filter) over a bowl. Pour liquid through the cloth to strain. Set liquid aside. In a large, heavy skillet melt butter. Add porcini and shitake mushrooms. Season with salt and sauté for 10 minutes or until golden brown. Add shallots and continue to sauté for 2 minutes. Add brandy and the reserved liquid. Bring to a boil and cook for 3 minute or until liquid is absorbed. Add 1 tablespoon thyme and stir to combine. Remove from heat and set aside to cool.

To assemble tart, preheat oven to 375 degrees. Sprinkle one-half of the cheese on top of baked crust. Top with mushroom mixture, spreading out evenly to edges. In a small bowl add cream, egg, egg yolks and remaining one tablespoon thyme. Whisk to combine and immediately pour over the top of the mushrooms. Top with the remaining one-half of cheese. Place in oven and bake for 30 minutes or until top is golden. Remove from oven and cool on a wire rack for 15 minutes. Serve warm. Makes 8 to 12 servings.

Broccoli Soufflé

Chef Gary Hild has a way with vegetables. He transforms fresh and seasonal gems into those dishes that you go back to over and over. This one is a simple soufflé that would be perfect for a brunch or as a side dish.

1 gallon water
1 teaspoon salt
1 pound broccoli florets, fresh, washed
3 large eggs
½ cup heavy cream
½ cup parmesan cheese, freshly grated
¾ cup bread crumbs
1 teaspoon salt
½ teaspoon white ground pepper
Butter, for baking pan and parchment paper

Preheat oven to 350 degrees. In a large pot add water and salt. Bring to a boil over medium-high heat. Add broccoli and cook for 8 minutes or until bright green color and still a little firm. Remove from heat and drain through a colander. Immediately transfer to a bowl with ice and water to stop cooking process. Set aside. In a food processor add eggs, cream, cheese, bread crumbs, salt, and pepper. Puree and set aside. Drain cooled broccoli in colander and transfer to a large bowl. Add puree mixture and gently stir to combine. Equally divide the soufflé mixture into the muffin cups that have been lightly buttered, filling them to the top. Place a sheet of parchment paper on top, be sure to butter it also so buttered side touches soufflé. Place a sheet pan on top of the parchment paper. Place in oven and bake for 20 minutes or until instant-read thermometer reads 350 degrees when inserted into the center of soufflé. Remove from oven and set aside on a wire rack to rest for a few minutes. Serve warm. Makes 12 servings.

Etc.

Including a bit of broccoli stem with the florets actually adds texture as well as flavor. When weighing the one pound of florets for this recipe feel free to substitute up to 4 ounces of broccoli stem, if desired.

Lesson Seven

Breads

Apricot Croissants

Buttermilk Cheddar Biscuits

The Culinary Center's Focaccia Dough

Irish Brown Bread

English Digestive Biscuits With Blue Cheese Brandy Butter

Weekend Morning Currant Scones

Apricot Croissants

When Connie Green, owner of Western Way Bed & Breakfast in Kearney, Missouri, shared this recipe with her class entitled "Bed and Breakfast Fare," we honestly didn't know whether it should be served as bread or as a dessert. Once they tasted it, everyone raved. So, in the end, no one really cared what category it fit into – they just wanted more!

Butter, for baking dish
6 croissants, fresh
1 (9-ounce) jar apricot preserves
6 tablespoons orange juice, fresh (or bottled)
5 large eggs
1 cup heavy cream
1 teaspoon almond extract

6 teaspoons raspberry preserves, for garnish

Preheat oven to 350 degrees. Butter a 9" x 13" ovenproof baking dish. Using a sharp knife, cut croissants in half, lengthwise, and line the bottoms only in dish. Set tops aside. In a small bowl add apricot preserves and juice. Stir to combine and spoon over croissants in dish, saving a little to be used as a glaze. Replace the tops. In a medium bowl add eggs, cream and almond extract. Stir to combine well. Pour liquid evenly over the top of croissants and spoon the remaining thinned preserves over top. Cover with plastic wrap and place in refrigerator overnight. Remove from refrigerator about 45 minutes before baking. Remove plastic wrap and place in oven. Bake for 30 to 35 minutes. Remove from oven. Spread raspberry preserves evenly over top, for garnish. Serve immediately. Makes 6 servings.

Buttermilk Cheddar Biscuits

Make 'em. Slather 'em with butter while they're warm. Eat 'em. This needs to be the plan.

4 ounces cake flour plus more for rolling and cutting
6 ounces bread flour
1 tablespoon plus 1 teaspoon baking powder
4-½ tablespoons sugar
2 teaspoons salt
½ cup butter, unsalted, cold, chopped
½ cup sharp cheddar cheese, grated
1 cup buttermilk

Preheat oven to 450 degrees. In a bowl add cake flour, bread flour, baking powder, sugar, and salt. Transfer to a sifter and sift into another mixing bowl. Using a pastry blender, cut butter into flour until mixture forms pea-size balls. Add the cheese and gently toss to combine. Using your fingers, make a well in the center of the dough and pour buttermilk inside. Using your hands, gently fold buttermilk into dough until all liquid is incorporated. Transfer to a lightly flour counter top. Using a rolling pin dusted in flour, roll dough out to ¾-inch thickness. Using a round cookie cutter dipped in flour, cut dough into rounds, being careful not to rotate the cutter. Transfer dough rounds to a baking sheet lined with parchment paper (or lightly sprayed with pan spray). Place in oven and bake for 10 to 15 minutes or until golden brown. Remove from oven and transfer to a serving plate or bowl. Cover with a towel to keep warm. Serve warm. Makes 7 to 8 biscuits.

Etc.

Originally, buttermilk was the liquid left behind after churning butter out of cream as is known as "traditional buttermilk." Cultured buttermilk is produced from cow's milk and has a characteristically sour taste caused by lactic acid bacteria. The latter is used in this recipe.

The Culinary Center's Focaccia Dough

We have several focaccia doughs that we use here at The Culinary Center. This is one that we have used for 15 years so you know it works!

5-½ tablespoons water (at 100 degrees)
½ teaspoon dry active yeast
½ tablespoon olive oil plus more for baking
1 teaspoon honey
Pinch of salt plus more for baking
Pinch of freshly ground white pepper
*   plus more for baking*
1-⅛ cups all-purpose flour plus more for rolling
Oil, for bowl
Cornmeal, for baking sheet
2 to 3 tablespoons rosemary, fresh, chopped
2 to 3 tablespoons Asiago cheese (or parmesan), grated
1 large egg, lightly beaten

Preheat oven to 450 degrees. Fit electric mixer with whisk attachment. In an electric mixer bowl add water, yeast, oil, honey, salt and pepper. Mix on low until yeast is dissolved. Replace whisk with dough hook attachment. Reduce speed to low and gradually add flour. Mix until dough pulls away from the sides of the bowl; then turn speed up to medium and continue to mix for 7 minutes. Remove dough from bowl and transfer to a lightly greased bowl. Cover bowl loosely with plastic wrap (or a towel). Set aside in a warm area until dough doubles in size.

Remove cover and punch the dough down with your fist. Remove dough and divide into 2 pieces. Using your hands, roll each dough to make a nice, round ball. On a lightly floured flat surface (or pastry cloth), add 1 dough ball and sprinkle with flour. Using a lightly floured rolling pin, roll the dough out to about ½-inch thickness. Transfer to a baking sheet dusted with cornmeal. Repeat process for second dough ball. Using a pastry brush, lightly coat the top of dough with oil. Lightly sprinkle top of dough with salt, pepper, rosemary, and cheese. Cover pan with a sheet of plastic wrap (or towel) and set aside to rise for 15 minutes so it can recover its size before baking.

Place in oven for 8 minutes. Open oven and brush top of focaccia with egg to glaze. Continue to bake for 2 minutes or until golden brown. Remove from oven and set aside to cool for several minutes. To serve cut in wedges or slices. Serve warm or at room temperature. Makes one small focaccia sheet.

Irish Brown Bread

On a culinary trip to Ireland, I made it my quest to find the recipe for the perfect Irish brown bread. The original form of this recipe was written in a taxi on the edge of a newspaper. It was dictated to me in heavy Irish brogue by a woman who lived on an island off the coast of Ireland. Doesn't get any more authentic than this! I brought it home, tested it and created this recipe. Enjoy!

1-¾ cup whole wheat ("whole meal") flour
1-¾ cup all-purpose flour, plus more for rolling
1 teaspoon salt
1 teaspoon baking soda
3 to 5 tablespoons mixed seeds, whole
    (pumpkin, sesame, sunflower, chia, flax, etc.)
2 tablespoons butter, unsalted, room temperature
1 large egg
1-⅔ cup buttermilk, divided

Preheat oven to 425 degrees. In a large bowl sift together both flours, salt, and baking soda. Add seeds and gently stir to combine. Using fingertips, rub butter into the flour mixture just until the texture resembles bread crumbs. Do not over-mix. Make a well in the center. Set aside. In another bowl add egg and buttermilk. Whisk together to combine. Pour 1-1/3 cups of the buttermilk into the well in flour mixture.

Using one hand with your fingers outstretched like a claw, bring the flour and liquid together until dough is quite soft, but not too sticky (adding the remaining 1/3 cup buttermilk, a little at a time, if necessary). Turn the dough onto a clean flat surface lightly dusted with flour. Using your hands (or rolling pin dusted with flour), gently press (or roll) the dough together into a round about 1-1/2 inches thick. (Do not over-handle.) Carefully transfer the dough to a large ungreased baking sheet. Using a sharp knife, score a deep cross on top of the loaf. Place in the oven and bake for 15 minutes.

Lower the oven temperature to 400 degrees and continue to bake for 30 minutes or until you hear a slightly hollow sound when tapping on the bottom of the loaf with a spoon (or your fingers). Remove from the oven and transfer loaf to a wire rack to cool. Serve warm with butter (preferably Irish butter!) Makes one loaf.

Etc.

Wholemeal flour is the name used in the UK for flours that contain all the bran and germ. The quality of the UK's version of whole wheat flour is often considered better than the more commercial machine-made "whole wheat" produced in the U.S. If you're lucky enough to find Irish "whole meal" flour here in the U.S., then use it!

English Digestive Biscuits With Blue Cheese Brandy Butter

We were introduced to these treats, essentially home-made graham crackers, by our first Executive Chef Nancy Stark. They were a staple for our appetizers receptions in the early years. They remain a timeless recipe.

BISCUITS
½ cup all-purpose flour, unbleached, plus more for kneading and rolling (preferably King Arthur)
1-½ cups whole wheat flour, stone ground (preferably King Arthur)
1 teaspoon baking powder
½ cup butter, unsalted, cold
¾ cup powdered sugar
½ cup whole milk, cold
Spray oil, for baking sheet

BUTTER
6 tablespoons blue cheese (use a fine English stilton, if possible)
3 tablespoons butter, unsalted, room temperature
1 tablespoon brandy
Freshly ground black pepper to taste

For the biscuits, in a mixing bowl add both flours, and baking powder. With a large wooden spoon, gently toss to combine. Add butter. Using a pastry blender (or 2 knifes or your fingertips), cut (or rub) butter into the flour mixture until it forms small pea-size balls. Add sugar and milk. Using a large wood spoon (or your hands), mix together until just combined. Turn the dough onto a lightly floured flat surface (or pastry cloth). Using your hands, knead until dough is smooth, being careful not to over-mix. (All this can be done almost instantly in a food processor, if desired.) Place dough back into the bowl and cover with a piece of plastic wrap. Place in refrigerator for 1 hour to chill. (This resting time will make the biscuits more tender and crisp but if you don't have the time, you may skip this step.) When dough has chilled, preheat oven to 350 degrees.

Lightly coat a large baking sheet with spray oil. Remove dough from refrigerator and place on a lightly floured flat surface (or pastry cloth). Using a rolling pin that has been lightly dusted with flour, roll the dough out until it is a bit more than 1/8-inch thick. Using a cookie cutter dipped in flour, cut the dough into any desired shape. (Traditionally these biscuits are about 2-1/2-inches round but creating small square biscuits makes easy work of the cutting process.) Transfer the biscuits to the baking sheet. Using a fork, prick the surface of each biscuit evenly around entire top. Place in oven for 15 to 20 minutes or until crisp and a pale, gold color. Remove from oven and set aside to cool for about 5 minutes. Transfer to a wire rack to cool completely. (The biscuits may be stored in an air-tight container for up to 1 week.)

For the butter, place all ingredients in a food processor. Process until well combined, scraping sides frequently. Spoon into a piping bag fitted with a star tip. Pipe onto biscuits.

Weekend Morning Currant Scones

Scones are sweet, rich biscuits that are usually made with cream as well as butter. There is nothing better than whipping up a batch of these on a weekend morning. Serve with a smile ... and coffee.

2 cups all-purpose flour plus more for shaping
⅓ cup sugar
1 tablespoon baking powder
½ teaspoon salt
6 tablespoons butter, unsalted, cold, cut into pieces
½ cup dried currants (or raisins)
1 large egg
½ cup heavy cream
1 teaspoon orange zest, freshly grated (optional)
2 to 3 teaspoons whole milk (or cream)
Cinnamon and sugar, for sprinkling (optional)

Preheat oven to 425 degrees. In a large bowl add flour, sugar, baking powder, and salt. Whisk together until well combined. Add butter. Using a pastry blender (or 2 knives), quickly toss the butter with the flour mixture to coat and separate them as you work, being careful not to allow the butter to melt or form a paste with the flour. (Largest pieces should be the size of peas and the rest resemble breadcrumbs.) Add currants. Using a large wooden spoon, gently stir to combine. Set aside. In a small bowl add egg, cream, and orange zest. Whisk to combine and pour into the dough mixture. Using a rubber spatula (or wooden spoon or fork), gently mix the dough until the dry ingredients are moistened. While still in the bowl, gather the dough and knead it gently against the sides and bottom of bowl 5 to 10 times, using your hands. (Turn and press any loose pieces into the dough each time until they adhere and the bowl is fairly clean.) Transfer the dough to a lightly floured flat surface (or pastry cloth). Dip your fingers in flour and pat the dough into an 8-inch round that is about 3/4-inch thick. Using a sharp knife, cut the dough into 8 to 12 wedges and transfer to a large ungreased baking sheet, placing at least ½-inch apart. Using a pastry brush, lightly coat the tops of scones with the milk and sprinkle with cinnamon and sugar. Place in oven and bake for 12 to 15 minutes or until tops are golden brown. Remove from oven and transfer to a wire rack to cool. Serve warm. Makes 8 large (or 12 small) scones.

Lesson Eight

Desserts

Ami-Grammer's Old-Fashioned Apple Pie

Blueberry Citrus Tart

Chipotle Brownies

Chocolate Pepper Cookies

Choco-Cappuccino Shortbread Cookies

Dokey's Coconut Dream Pie

Ginger Blueberry Crème Brûlée

Lavender Pound Cake

Luscious Berry Dessert "Soup"

Milk Chocolate Hazelnut Crème Brûlée

Our Favorite Italian Biscotti

"Pumpkin Pie" Cake

Spanish Churros With Chocolate Dipping Sauce

Strawberries in Peppered Red Wine Sauce

Your New Favorite Cookie

Ami-Grammer's Old-Fashioned Apple Pie

A tribute to my Ami-Grammers (a/k/a grandmother) who taught me how to make pies when I was so little I had to sit on the counter to watch. She was part of my inspiration to develop a culinary arts center! This is for you, Ami-Grammers!

PASTRY (for double crust)
4 cups all-purpose flour plus more for rolling
1 teaspoon salt
1-1/3 cups shortening, chilled
4 tablespoons butter, unsalted, chilled
8 to 10 tablespoons cold water

FILLING
6 cups (6 to 8 medium) tart cooking apples,
    cored, peeled, thinly sliced
1 tablespoon lemon juice, freshly squeezed
1 cup sugar plus more to taste, depending on
    tartness of apples
1/4 teaspoon salt
2 to 3 tablespoons all-purpose flour
    (or 1 to 2 tablespoons cornstarch)
3/4 teaspoon ground cinnamon
1/4 teaspoon ground nutmeg
1 teaspoon vanilla extract
4 tablespoons butter, unsalted, cut into small pieces,
    divided

TOPPING
1 tablespoon vanilla extract
1 tablespoon sugar
1 tablespoon ground cinnamon

Preheat oven to 450 degrees.

For the pastry, in a large bowl add flour and salt. Using a large spoon, gently mix together. Add shortening and butter. Using a pastry blender (or knife or your fingers), cut into flour mixture until it resembles coarse cornmeal. (Do not over-mix as pastry will become tough.) Sprinkle water over mixture, 2-4 tablespoons at a time, blending lightly with a fork after each addition. Repeat this process with remaining water, as needed, or until you can gather the dough into a tidy ball. Divide pastry in half and form each into a ball. On a lightly floured flat surface place one of the dough ball.

Etc.

To prevent pastry dough from shrinking during baking, wrap raw dough in plastic wrap and place in refrigerator for an hour or more. Remove from refrigerator and allow it to come to just below room temperature before rolling.

Using a floured rolling pin, flatten and roll into a rough 12-inch circle. Transfer to a 9-inch pie backing dish. Using fingers, lightly press into surface of dish leaving excess hanging over sides of dish. Repeat rolling process with second ball. Leave it to rest on surface until ready to top filling.

For the filling, in a large bowl add apples and sprinkle juice over top. Set aside. In a small bowl add sugar, salt, flour, cinnamon, nutmeg, and vanilla. (Only very juicy apples will require the larger amount of flour or cornstarch.) Using a large spoon, stir to combine. Add sugar mix to the apples and gently stir until all are coated. Transfer filling to the pastry-lined pie dish and dot with 2 tablespoons butter. Top with second pastry round. Trim both doughs to about ½-inch beyond the edge of pie dish. Using your fingers, seal by rolling dough under and pressing and crimping lightly until entire pie is sealed. Dot the top of the pie with the remaining 2 tablespoons butter. Using a fork, prick holes about 3 to 4 times around top of pie to allow steam to escape during baking.

For the topping, sprinkle vanilla over top of pie. In a small bowl add sugar and cinnamon. Stir to combine and sprinkle mixture evenly over crust.

Place pie in oven and bake for 10 minutes. Reduce the heat to 350 degrees and continue to bake for 35 to 40 minutes or until golden brown. (Do not over-bake. As pie cools the filling will set slightly.) Remove from oven to a wire rack to cool. Serve warm. Makes 8 servings.

Blueberry Citrus Tart

This is one of the first desserts we developed for use at The Culinary Center's caterings and in classes. It has withstood the test of time! The combination of the blueberries and lemon juice makes a refreshing and light ending to a meal. Cut into interesting shapes like triangles or tiny squares and serve topped with citrus zest and a dusting of powdered sugar. Makes a "homey" recipe come across most elegant!

Oil, for pan
1 cup butter, unsalted, room temperature
¾ cup powdered sugar plus more, for garnish, sifted, divided
2-¼ cups all-purpose flour, divided
4 large eggs
1-½ cups sugar
⅓ cup lemon juice, freshly squeezed
2 tablespoons lemon zest, freshly grated
1 teaspoon baking powder
1-½ cups blueberries, fresh, washed, drained
Fresh lemon (or orange) peel curls, for garnish

Preheat oven to 350 degrees. Lightly oil a 9" x 13" baking pan. In an electric mixer bowl add butter and powdered sugar. Cream until smooth. Add 2 cups flour and continue to mix until well blended. Transfer mixture to the baking pan. Using fingers (or the back of a spoon), press mixture into bottom of pan. Place in oven and bake for 20 minutes or until golden. Remove from oven and set on a wire rack to cool.

In a second mixing bowl add eggs, sugar, juice, zest, remaining ¼-cup flour, and baking powder. Beat on high speed for 2 minutes, scraping sides to incorporate all ingredients. Transfer mixture to the baking pan with crust and spread evenly to the sides of the pan. Sprinkle the berries evenly on top of the batter. Place in oven and bake for 30 to 35 minutes or until light brown and set. Remove from oven and place on wire rack to cool completely. Using a sharp knife, cut tart into triangles (or bars). Place on an individual dessert plate. Sprinkle powdered sugar on top just before serving. Top with a lemon or orange curl, for garnish. Serve at room temperature. Serves 12 to 16.

Etc.

Frozen blueberries can also be used to create a welcome "summery" dessert in the cold winter months. Just make sure to defrost and drain the liquid before use.

Chipotle Brownies

Chocolate and chilies! In case you didn't know, they've been combining the two south of the border for centuries. Can you say "mole sauce!" Anyway, here the two are combined in a dessert that is very unique. Great paired with a bbq or smoked menu. The quality of this dish is without doubt dependent on the quality of chocolate used!

½ pound semisweet chocolate, broken into chunks
¾ pound butter, unsalted
7 large eggs
1-½ pounds sugar
½ cup cocoa powder, dark
2 tablespoons canned chipotle chilies
    in adobo sauce, pureed
¼ teaspoon salt
1 tablespoon vanilla extract
2-½ cups all-purpose flour,
    sifted plus more for pan
8 ounces walnuts (or pecans), chopped
Oil, for pan

Preheat oven to 350 degrees. In a double boiler over low heat add chocolate and butter. Allow mixture to melt together, stirring occasionally. Remove from heat and set aside to cool to room temperature. In a large mixing bowl add eggs, sugar, cocoa, chilie puree, salt, and vanilla. Using an electric hand mixer on medium, mix well. (Do not whip.) Add chocolate mixture and blend to combine. Fold in flour and nuts. Lightly grease and flour a 17" x 13" jelly roll pan. Transfer batter into pan and bake for 35 to 40 minutes or until toothpick inserted in center comes out clean. Serve warm. Makes about 24 to 36 large brownies OR about 100 forkfuls as you pass through the kitchen.

Etc.

A chipotle (or chilpotle) comes from the Nahuatl word "chilpoctli" meaning "smoked chili." It is a smoked-dried jalapeno. Chipotles in adobo sauce means that the smoked jalapeno is then cooked in a tomato style sauce. The latter can be found canned and in most grocery stores in the ethnic food section.

Chocolate Pepper Cookies

These are some of our favorite cookies because they are not so sweet and have just a hint of "bite" from the pepper. We recommend them often for wedding, showers and anniversaries as they make an elegant and dramatic presentation.

COOKIES
1 pound butter, unsalted, room temperature
2-¼ cups sugar, divided
2 teaspoons vanilla extract
4 large egg yolks plus 1 egg, lightly beaten
1 teaspoon ground black pepper or to taste
4 cups all-purpose flour plus more for rolling
½ teaspoon baking powder
1 cup cocoa powder
½ teaspoon salt
2 cups almonds, lightly toasted, cooled, ground

GANACHE
1-½ cups heavy cream
22 ounces semisweet chocolate
3 tablespoons butter, unsalted
2 ounces flavored liqueur (optional)

For the cookies, preheat oven to 350 degrees. In an electric mixer bowl add butter and 2 cups of sugar. Cream ingredients together at medium to high speed, scraping sides of bowl as needed. Add vanilla and eggs, one at a time, beating well after each addition. Using a sifter, in separate bowl sift together the pepper, flour, baking powder, cocoa, and salt. Add the sifted ingredients to the egg mixture and beat for one minute or just until well mixed, scraping sides to incorporate all of the dough. Add the almonds and mix for 30 seconds or until well combined, scraping sides. Divide the dough in half and form each into a ball. Wrap in plastic wrap and place in refrigerator for at least one hour or until well chilled. Remove from refrigerator and transfer to a countertop dusted with flour. With a floured rolling pin, roll dough to about ¼-inch thickness. Using a cookie cutter, cut dough into heart-shaped cookies (or shape of your choice) and transfer to an ungreased baking tray. Bake for 10 to 12 minutes or until light golden color. Do not over bake. Remove from oven and transfer to a wire rack to cool completely.

For the ganache, in a saucepan add cream and briefly bring to a boil over medium-high heat, stirring constantly to prevent scorching. Remove from heat and add chocolate. Cover tightly with lid and set aside for 5 minutes or until the chocolate has melted completely. Remove cover and stir in

Etc.

Ganache (pronounced "guh-NAWSH) is a mixture made of chocolate and cream (and sometimes eggs). While bittersweet chocolate is the chocolate used most in this classic recipe, white chocolate and milk chocolate may be substituted. This delicious cream is delicious on its own but for an extra surprise, can also be flavored with your choice of liqueur, especially when making truffles.

butter until melted and just combined. Add liqueur and stir to combine. Transfer ganache to an air-tight container and place in refrigerator until needed. (Ganache may be made ahead of time and kept in refrigerator for up to 2 weeks.) Makes 2-1/2 to 3 cups.

To assemble, spread a bit of ganache on the bottom of one cookie. Top with another cookie to form a sandwich. Makes 75 sandwich cookies (or 150 single cookies).

Choco-Cappuccino Shortbread Cookies

A "not too sweet" cookie that makes a great addition to your usual repertoire of favorite cookie recipes.

1 cup butter, unsalted, room temperature
½ cup sugar
4 teaspoons instant coffee, finely crushed
½ teaspoon vanilla extract
1-¾ cups all-purpose flour
¼ cup cornstarch
Oil, for baking sheet
6 (1-ounce) squares high quality
   semi-sweet chocolate, melted

Preheat oven to 325 degrees. In a large mixing bowl add butter and sugar. Beat on high speed until mixed together thoroughly. Add coffee and vanilla. Beat in to combine. Sift the flour and cornstarch together into another bowl. Gradually add into the butter mixture a little at a time, mixing well between each addition. Lightly grease a baking sheet. Using a tablespoon, remove dough one tablespoon at a time. Using your fingers, mold the dough into the shape of a coffee bean and place on the baking sheet, 2 inches apart. Repeat process until all dough is used. With a butter knife, gently press an indent of about 1/8-inch deep, lengthwise, on each cookie. (Makes it look more like an actual coffee bean.) Place in oven and bake for 15 minutes or until golden brown. Remove from oven and transfer cookies to a wire rack to cool completely. Meanwhile, in a bowl add melted chocolate. Place a sheet of waxed paper on the cooled baking sheet. Dip either one-half or both ends of cooled cookies into the chocolate and place on the cookie sheet. Place in refrigerator to cool chocolate completely. Remove from refrigerator and transfer cookies to an air-tight container. Store in a cool place for up to 2 weeks. Makes about 18 cookies, depending on size.

Etc.

For a great gift idea, tuck some of these inside a coffee mug and "wrap" with a beautiful cotton tea towel tied with a ribbon or raffia.

Dokey's Coconut Dream Pie

My Mom's name is Doris but her siblings refer to her as "Doke" or "Dokey." Growing up she always asked us what kind of cake we wanted for our birthdays. I always chose coconut cream pie! She makes the best!

CRUST
1 (10-ounce) box shortbread cookies
   (such as Lorna Doone)
1 cup sweetened coconut flakes
½ cup butter, unsalted, melted

FILLING
3 cups "half and half"
2 (4-serving) boxes instant vanilla pudding mix
1 cup sweetened coconut flakes
½ cup crushed pineapple, well drained
3 cups heavy whipping cream, divided

*Sweetened coconut flakes, toasted,
   cooled, for garnish*

For the crust, preheat oven to 350 degrees. In a large re-sealable plastic bag add cookies and close seal. Using the flat side of a meat mallet, pound cookies until they form crumbs. Transfer crumbs to a large mixing bowl. Add coconut and butter. Using a large wooden spoon, mix together until crumbs are well coated. In a 9-inch deep pie plate add crumbs and press into the bottom and sides of the entire plate, using your fingers. Place in the oven and bake for 10 minutes or until crust is browned. Remove from oven and transfer to a wire rack to cool while you prepare the filling.

For the filling, in a large mixing bowl add "half and half," and pudding mix. Using a large whisk, combine ingredients until well mixed and a thick texture. Add coconut. Using a large spoon, gently stir to combine thoroughly. Transfer the filling into the prepared crust. Using a butter knife (or cake knife or spatula), smooth filling so that is covers the entire pie plate. Place in refrigerator, uncovered, to chill until firm. In a bowl add drained pineapple. Using a paper towel, blot the pineapple to make sure that all liquid is absorbed and it is as dry as possible. (This is an important step as cream will not set well if pineapple is too wet.) Set aside. In a mixing bowl add cream. Mix on high speed until cream is thick. Transfer 1 cup of whipped cream to a separate bowl and set side. Gently fold the pineapple into the remaining whipped cream.

To assemble, carefully add the cream and pineapple mixture to the top of the pie and spread out to the edges of pan. Add the remaining 1 cup whipped cream to the top of the pie. Gently spread out to cover entire pie. Place in refrigerator, uncovered until well chilled. When ready to serve, remove from refrigerator. Sprinkle toasted coconut flakes over top of entire pie, for garnish. Serve chilled. Makes 8 to 10 servings.

Ginger Blueberry Crème Brûlée

If you are one for drama, instead of broiling the sugar at the end of this recipe, you could grab your handy dandy blow torch and caramelize these at the table. Yes, that's what we said.....a blow torch. Kitchenware stores carry small "kitchen-size" blow torches but there's nothing wrong with the manly version you purchase at the hardware store – and it's a lot cheaper...not to mention infinitely more impressive!

4 cups heavy cream
½ cup ginger, fresh, peeled, finely chopped
Salt to taste
8 large eggs yolks
¾ cup plus 2 tablespoons sugar
½ cup dried blueberries (or 1 cup fresh blueberries, washed, drained)
4 teaspoons crystallized ginger, chopped
Hot water, for baking
16 teaspoons turbinado sugar

Preheat oven to 300 degrees. In a medium saucepan add cream, fresh ginger, and salt. Cook over medium heat until the surface begins to shimmer, stirring constantly to prevent scorching. Remove from heat, cover and set aside for 30 minutes to infuse flavors.

In a large heatproof bowl add yolks and sugar. Using a wooden spoon, stir until mixture is blended together and sugar is dissolved. Slowly add in cream mixture while stirring gently until custard is formed. Carefully pour into a large measuring cup and skim off any bubbles. Set aside.

In a large roasting pan place 8 shallow (4-1/2 inch-wide) ramekins. Add the blueberries and crystallized ginger by dividing each evenly between the ramekins. Slowly pour the custard into the ramekins, filling them almost to the top. Place roasting pan in the center of the oven and carefully enough hot water to reach halfway up the sides of the ramekins. Cover the pan loosely with a sheet of aluminum foil and bake for 1 hour or until custards are firm at the edges but still a bit wobbly in the center. Remove the ramekins from the oven and transfer to a wire rack to cool completely. (For safety, turn off oven and allow baking sheet with water to cool before removing from oven.) Cover with plastic wrap and refrigerate for 3 hours (or up to 2 days) until cold.

To serve, preheat the broiler. Remove custards from refrigerator and transfer to a baking sheet. Using a paper towel, carefully blot the surfaces of custards to remove any condensation. Using a small sieve, sift 2 teaspoons of the turbinado sugar over top of each custard in a thin, even layer. Place sheet in oven and broil the custards as close to the heat as possible for 30 seconds to 2 minutes or until sugar is evenly caramelized. Remove from oven and place on a wire rack to cool slightly. Serve immediately. Makes 8 servings.

Lavender Pound Cake

An impressive quick bread that is perfectly paired with fresh berries and freshly whipped cream. Dust with some powdered sugar for an elegant presentation. One of my favorite recipes of all time!

Oil, for pan
3-½ cups all-purpose flour plus
*   more for dusting baking pan*
2 teaspoons baking powder
2-½ cups butter, room temperature
12 large eggs, separated, divided
2-½ cups sugar
2 tablespoons sweet sherry
1 tablespoon dried lavender flower
*   (or 2 tablespoons fresh)*

Preheat oven to 325 degrees. Prepare a 10" tube pan (or bundt pan) by greasing well and dusting with flour. Set aside.   In a bowl add flour and baking powder. Gently stir to combine. Set aside. In a mixing bowl add butter. Using a hand mixer, cream on high speed until light and fluffy, scraping sides of bowl with a spatula, as needed. Add flour mix, a little at a time, and beat until dough is a smooth paste, scraping sides of bowl often. Set aside. In a separate large mixing bowl, add egg yolks and sugar. Using an electric mixer with clean beaters, beat until mixture is thick and light. Add sherry and lavender and mix to combine. Add butter and flour mixture, a little at a time, and beat until combined thoroughly, scraping sides as needed to incorporate all ingredients. Set aside. In another mixing bowl add egg whites. Using electric mixer with clean beaters, beat egg whites on high speed until stiff peaks form but are not dry. Using a spatula, quickly and gently fold whites into the dough. Turn batter into the baking pan and place in the oven. Bake for 1 hour and 15 minutes or until straw (or knife) inserted in cake comes out clean. Remove from oven and transfer to a wire rack to cool. Serve. Makes 8 to 12 servings.

Etc.

Did you know that many fresh flowers are edible as long as they are grown in an organic environment? They are often used by executive chefs in recipes for some of the most elegant, upscale restaurants. Lavender – a close cousin to the mint family - is a very versatile herb that lends a wonderfully aromatic flavor beautifully to baked goods, salads and entrees. Chefs often combine it with other fresh herbs such as rosemary, fennel and sage.

Luscious Berry Dessert "Soup"

Is it a cold soup or a dessert? You decide.

2 cups Pinot Noir (or other similar red wine)
1 cup water
⅔ cup sugar
¼ cup lemon juice, freshly squeezed
2 cinnamon sticks
12 ounces strawberries, fresh, washed, dried, small dice
¾ cup raspberries, fresh, divided (or frozen, thawed)
¾ cup blueberries, fresh, washed, dried, divided (or frozen, thawed)
¾ cup blackberries, fresh, washed, dried, divided (or frozen, thawed)
1 pint vanilla bean ice cream

1 cup of crème fraiche, for garnish

In a heavy, large saucepan add wine, water, sugar, juice and cinnamon sticks. Add ¼ cup each of strawberries, raspberries, blueberries, and blackberries. Stir to combine. Bring raspberries to a simmer over medium-high heat. Reduce the heat to medium-low and simmer gently for 10 minutes or until fruit is very tender. Remove from heat and set aside to cool slightly. Using a slotted spoon, remove the cinnamon sticks and discard. Transfer the cooled berry mixture to a blender and puree until smooth. Using a fine mesh strainer, strain the soup into a medium bowl. Cover with plastic wrap and refrigerate until very cold. (This soup is best made a day ahead, if possible.) To serve, using a sharp knife, cut the remaining reserved berries into small pieces. For a dessert, in decorative dessert glasses (or soup bowls), place a small scoop of the ice cream in the center. Pour the equal portions of the soup around the ice cream in each glass. Sprinkle with the reserved berries, for garnish. Serve cold. For a cold soup, ladle soup into bowls and top with a dollop of crème fraiche and berry pieces. Makes 8 servings.

Soups are one of life's simple pleasures. Summer soups such as gazpacho, cold cucumber soup, and fresh berry soups make perfect use of the bounty of ripe, juicy fruits and vegetables available at your local farmers markets.

Milk Chocolate Hazelnut Crème Brûlée

A beautiful use of a time-honored ingredient known as "Nutella." The Europeans have enjoyed Nutella for years in the same way we have enjoyed peanut butter here "across the pond!"

CUSTARD
4 cups heavy cream
1 vanilla bean, split lengthwise
Pinch of salt
8 large egg yolks
¾ cup plus 2 tablespoons sugar
½ cup Nutella brand chocolate-hazelnut spread
    (found in major grocery stores in baking aisle)
Water, for baking

GLAZE
16 teaspoons sugar, divided

For the custard, Preheat oven to 300 degrees. In a medium saucepan add cream, vanilla bean, and salt. Heat over medium heat until surface of liquid begins to shimmer, stirring constantly to prevent scorching. Remove from heat and set aside. In a large heatproof bowl, add egg yolks and sugar. With a wooden spoon, stir until combined. Slowly add the hot cream mixture into egg mixture, stirring gently. Add Nutella and stir to combine. With a mesh sieve, strain the custard into a large heatproof measuring cup. Using a spoon, skim off any bubbles on top of custard. Set aside. In a shallow roasting pan arrange 8 oven-safe ramekins. Slowly pour the custard into the ramekins, dividing evenly. Place the pan in the center of the oven. Carefully pour in enough water to reach halfway up the sides of the ramekins to form a water bath. Cover the pan loosely with a sheet of aluminum foil and bake for 1 hour or until the custards are firm at the edges, but still a bit wobbly in the center. Carefully remove from oven and transfer the ramekins to a wire rack to cool completely. Cover each with a sheet of plastic wrap and refrigerate at least 3 hours or until cold. (Custards may be made ahead and kept in refrigerator for up to 2 days.)

For the glaze, preheat the broiler. Remove the custards from the refrigerator at least 1 hour before ready to serve. Sprinkle 2 teaspoons sugar over each custard in a thin, even layer and place on a baking sheet. Place sheet in the oven to broil as close to the heat as possible for 30 seconds to 2 minutes or until the sugar is evenly caramelized, watching closely so they don't burn. Remove from oven and transfer ramekins to a wire rack to cool slightly. Serve immediately. Makes 8 servings.

Etc.

Crème Brûlée (also known as Trinity cream or burnt cream), is an elegant custard-based dessert that is topped with a caramelized sugar "crust." Break out the blow torch instead of broiling and look like a superhero to your guest... but for heaven's sake be careful!

Our Favorite Italian Biscotti

These "twice baked" Italian cookies are much easier to make than most people think. They are meant to be dipped into coffee or a dessert wine (such as Vin Santo or "holy wine"). We demonstrate this recipe quite often at our very popular classes focusing on the foods of Italy, especially the region of Tuscany.

2 large eggs, whole, plus 1 large egg,
    lightly beaten, divided
1 large egg yolk
1 teaspoon vanilla extract
2 teaspoons orange (or lemon) zest, freshly grated
2 cups unbleached all-purpose flour
1 cup sugar
1 teaspoon baking powder
1/4 teaspoon baking soda
1/8 teaspoon salt
1/2 cup almonds, whole, toasted, chopped
1/2 cup pistachio nuts, unsalted, toasted, chopped
3 tablespoons butter, unsalted, room temperature
Sugar, for sprinkling

Preheat oven to 350 degrees. In a small bowl add 2 eggs, egg yolk, vanilla, and zest. Using a fork, beat lightly. Set aside. In a large mixing bowl add flour, sugar, baking powder, baking soda, salt, almonds, pistachio nuts, and butter. Using an electric hand mixer set to medium speed, mix together until combined. Add egg mixture and continue to mix together until a granular dough forms. (This dough may over-tax the motor of some hand-held mixers. If it does, beat the mixture only until it is a rough, shaggy mass. Then dust hands with flour and knead in the bowl until all ingredients are well incorporated.) Turn out the dough onto a clean, lightly floured countertop. Using hands, knead dough for about one minute. Divide the dough into 4 equal portions. Using the palms of your hand, roll each portion into a log about 12-inches long and 1-inch in diameter. Transfer logs to a 12" x 15" baking sheet lined with parchment paper (or greased with butter) by placing crosswise on the sheet and spacing them about 2-inches apart. Using the palm of one hand, lightly flatten the top of each log until it is about 1/2-inch thick. Set aside.

Using a pastry brush, paint logs with the remaining lightly beaten egg and sprinkle with sugar.

Place logs in the oven and bake for 15 to 20 minutes or until golden brown. Remove from the oven and let cool on the baking sheet for about 10 minutes or until they can be safely handled. (Leave oven set at 350 degrees.) Transfer logs to a clean cutting board. Using a sharp knife, cut each log cross-wise on the diagonal into ½-inch wide pieces. On a second baking sheet lined with parchment paper, transfer biscottis, cut side down, on the sheet. Place in oven and continue to bake for another 10 minutes or until lightly toasted and the edges are golden brown. Remove from oven and allow to cool on the baking sheet for 10 minutes or until completely cooled. Serve immediately (or store in a covered container at room temperature for up to 2 weeks). Makes about 3 dozen biscotti.

"Pumpkin Pie" Cake

This easy and delicious dessert is a whole new take on a Thanksgiving holiday favorite! Try making cupcakes with this recipe for an unique updated "smallcake" treat. Why not top with a tiny candy pumpkin?

Oil, for pan
1 (32-ounce) can pure pumpkin
4 large eggs, lightly beaten
1 (12-ounce) can evaporated milk
1-½ cups sugar
2 teaspoons ground cinnamon
1 teaspoon ground nutmeg
⅓ teaspoon ground ginger
1 box yellow cake mix
¾ cup butter (or margarine), melted
½ cup walnuts, chopped

Preheat oven to 300 degrees. Lightly oil a 9" x 13" baking pan. In a large bowl add pumpkin, eggs, milk, sugar, cinnamon, nutmeg, and ginger. Using a large spoon, beat until combined thoroughly, scraping sides as needed. Pour into baking pan. Sprinkle dry cake mix evenly over the top of batter. Drizzle butter over cake mix and top with nuts, spreading both layers evenly to edges of pan. Place in oven and bake for 1 hour and 20 minutes or until knife inserted into center comes out clean. Remove from oven and set on a wire rack to cool before cutting. Serve warm. Makes 16 servings.

Etc.

For an extra special treat, add a dollop of cinnamon whipped cream on top of each serving. To make: in a small bowl add 1 cup whipping cream and beat until slightly thickened. Gradually blend in 2 to 4 table-spoons powdered sugar, ½ teaspoon vanilla, and ¼ teaspoon ground cinnamon. Beat until combined thoroughly and thickened. Makes 2 cups. For successful fluffy topping, be sure that whipping cream, bowl and beaters are chilled thoroughly. Don't overbeat or even-tually you'll have butter.

Spanish Churros With Chocolate Dipping Sauce

In 2006 I took a group of 19 to San Miguel de Allende, Mexico for a culinary tour. A memorable highlight was standing on the sidewalk watching churros being made through the window of a kitchen in the downtown area of this ancient walled city. The long thin strands of dough dropped into the hot oil, then dusted with sugar and cinnamon when they came out. Move over Dunkin' Donuts.

SAUCE
1 cup heavy cream
8 ounces dark chocolate, chopped
1 tablespoon coffee-flavored liqueur (such as Kahlua)

CHURROS
¼ cup sugar
¼ teaspoon ground cinnamon,
Vegetable oil (or olive oil), for frying
    (enough to fill pan to about 1-½ inches deep)
1 cup water
½ cup butter, unsalted, cut into chunks
¼ teaspoon salt
1 cup all-purpose flour
3 large eggs

For the sauce, in a small saucepan add cream and bring to a boil over high heat, stirring constantly to prevent scorching. Remove from heat and set aside. In a mixing bowl add chocolate. Pour warm cream over top and stir until well mixed and chocolate is completely melted. Add liqueur and stir to combine. Transfer to a serving bowl and set aside.

For the churros, in a small bowl add sugar and cinnamon. Stir to combine and set aside. In a deep fryer (or deep skillet) heat oil on high heat until it reaches 360 degrees on an instant-read thermometer. While oil is heating, in a 3-quart saucepan add water, butter, and salt. Bring to a boil over high heat, stirring occasionally; then reduce heat to low. Add flour and stir vigorously for 1 minute or until mixture forms a ball. Remove from heat. Using a large spoon, beat all eggs into the dough until mixture is smooth. In a pastry bag fitted with a large star tip, spoon dough in until half full. Remove the air from bag by twisting tightly. Carefully squeeze 4-inch strips directly into the hot oil, cutting pieces off with a butter knife after adding each strip. Fry for 2 minutes or until golden brown, turning once. Using a large slotted spoon (or tongs), gently skim churros out of oil and place on a plate lined with paper towels to drain. Repeat process until all pastry is used. Transfer churros to a serving platter and dust equal portions of sugar mixture over each. Serve immediately with chocolate sauce on the side, for dipping. Makes 4 servings.

Strawberries in Peppered Red Wine Sauce

I developed this recipe many years ago after tasting this unique dessert sauce at a favorite restaurant in Napa Valley, California. It took a while to figure out what the distinctive, and unexpected, flavor was in this complex-tasting dessert sauce. It was the peppercorns, of course! It is still a "go-to" recipe for me.

1 (750 ml.) bottle dry red wine
2 cups sugar
1 tablespoon lemon juice, freshly squeezed
Zest from 2 lemons
Zest from 2 oranges
2 cinnamon sticks, approximately 3-inches long
10 black peppercorns, whole (or more if you like)
Kosher salt to taste
2 quarts strawberries, fresh, washed,
    stems removed, sliced
Vanilla ice cream

In a heavy saucepan add wine, sugar, juice, zests, cinnamon sticks, peppercorns, and salt. Cook over medium high heat for 15 minutes or until sauce is reduced by at least one-half, stirring occasionally. Strain through a sieve into a serving bowl.

To serve, spoon strawberries and sauce over a good quality vanilla ice cream. Makes 8 servings.

Etc.

This sauce is very versatile. Drizzle it over pound cake or chocolate cake. Or reduce it even further, spoon sauce into a plastic squirt bottle, and use to decoratively "paint" dessert plates for an elegant presentation. Keeps well in the refrigerator for up to 3 -4 weeks. It also makes a thoughtful hostess or holiday gift when presented in a decorated jar or interesting container.

Your New Favorite Cookie

If you think the classic chocolate chip cookie can't be beat, just try these! 'Nuf said!

COOKIES
2-1/2 cups all-purpose flour
½ teaspoon baking soda
½ teaspoon salt
1 cup butter, unsalted, room temperature
1 cup sugar
½ cup brown sugar, packed
1 large egg
1 teaspoon orange zest, freshly grated
2 tablespoons orange juice
2 cups dried cranberries
½ cup pecans, coarsely chopped

GLAZE
1 cup powdered sugar
2 to 3 tablespoons orange juice
½ teaspoon orange zest, freshly grated

For the cookies, preheat oven to 375 degrees. In a bowl add flour, baking soda, and salt. Gently stir to combine. Set aside. In a mixing bowl add butter, sugar, and brown sugar. Using an electric mixer, cream together until smooth, scraping sides with a spatula, as needed. Add egg, zest, and juice. Mix together until well combined. Add flour mixture, a little at a time, and mix until all ingredients are thoroughly combined. Turn off mixer. Add cranberries and nuts. Using a large spoon, gently stir in until just combined. Do not over-mix. Using a tablespoon, spoon cookie dough onto a baking sheet lined with parchment paper, spacing at least 2-inches apart. Bake 10 to 12 minutes or until golden brown. Remove from the oven and set aside on baking sheet to cool. Using a spatula, gently remove cookies from baking sheet and transfer to a wire rack to cool completely. (These cookies will firm up when cooled.)

For the glaze, in a bowl add sugar, juice, and zest. Stir until smooth and combined. Drizzle over the top of cookies. Makes 4 dozen cookies.

Lesson Nine

Little Extras

Aioli

Asiago Alfredo Sauce

Basic Marinara Sauce

Basil Mint Sorbet

CCKC's Ginger Mint Tea

'Fire and Ice' Mango Sorbet

Fresh Fig Chutney

Lemongrass Sorbet

Sautéed Pineapple, Cucumber and Pine Nut Relish

Tomato Confiture

Aioli

A homemade aioli is excellent on its own or can be flavored in a variety of ways.

⅔ cup extra virgin olive oil
⅓ cup peanut oil (or canola oil)
4 large cloves garlic, fresh, peeled, minced
2 large egg yolks
4 teaspoons lemon juice, freshly squeezed
Kosher salt (or sea) to taste

In a measuring cup with a spout add olive and peanut oils. Set aside. In a blender add garlic, yolks, and juice. Pulse until mixture forms a coarse paste, scraping sides with a spatula as needed. With the motor running, add oil in a slow, thin, steady stream and blend until mixture is the consistency of a thick mayonnaise, scraping sides as needed. Transfer the aioli to a bowl, scraping sides with a spatula to remove thoroughly and season with salt. Cover bowl with a sheet of plastic wrap and place in refrigerator for at least 1 hour to chill before use. (Aioli may be kept in the refrigerator for up to one week.) Serve cold. Makes approximately 1 cup.

Asiago Alfredo Sauce

Northern Italian cuisine is known for its white sauces and there is no more beloved than a classic Alfredo sauce. This recipe would have the cook using only Asiago, an Italian cow's milk cheese, to give it a signature flavor. Asiago can vary from a smooth texture in its fresh state to a crumbly texture in the aged version. It is the aged version used in this recipe.

2-½ tablespoons cornstarch
2 tablespoons milk
1 quart heavy cream
3 cloves garlic, whole, roasted, peeled
¼ pound Asiago cheese, shredded
¾ teaspoon salt
¼ teaspoon freshly ground white pepper

In a small bowl add cornstarch and milk. Whisk briskly until mixture forms a slurry. Set aside. In a sauce pan on low heat add cream and garlic. Heat until cream is hot (but not boiling), stirring constantly to prevent scorching. Gradually mix in the cheese until melted, stirring constantly. Add slurry, salt and pepper. Whisk to combine well. Serve immediately over warm linguini or fettuccini pasta. Makes about 4 ½ cups.

Basic Marinara Sauce

Every seasoned chef or home-based cook should have a basic marinara sauce in their recipe box. This version of a quick red sauce uses canned tomatoes and dried herbs.

4 tablespoons olive oil
½ large onion, peeled, diced
2 tablespoons garlic cloves, fresh, peeled, finely minced
1 (24-ounce) can whole tomatoes, chopped
½ cup tomato paste
4 tablespoons basil, fresh, washed, dried, minced
2 tablespoons oregano, fresh, washed, dried, minced
2 tablespoons sugar
2 cups chicken stock
Kosher salt and coarsely ground black pepper to taste

In a 1-gallon stock pot heat oil for one minute over medium-high heat. Add onions and sweat for 1 to 2 minutes or until almost translucent, stirring occasionally. Add garlic and sauté for 2 to 3 minutes stirring constantly to prevent burning. Add tomatoes, tomato paste, basil, oregano, sugar, stock, salt, and pepper. Cook for 2 minutes, stirring frequently. Reduce heat to low and simmer sauce for 15 to 20 minutes or until sauce has thickened to desired consistency, stirring gently every 5 minutes or so. Remove from heat. To serve, ladle sauce over cooked pasta noodles. Serve warm. Makes 8 cups.

Etc.

If you want to really impress your family or guests, substitute vine-ripened Roma tomatoes that have been blanched, skinned and chopped along with fresh herbs from your garden. To save time, you can double or triple the recipe and freeze the leftovers in smaller portions to thaw for a quick weeknight dinner! Now, that's perfection!

Basil Mint Sorbet

This recipe was adapted from the Frances Mayes' popular book, "Under the Tuscan Sun," and is an excellent, low-fat way to savor two very special and prolific summer herbs. For a frosty and beautiful presentation, scoop the sorbet into clear glass dessert dishes and place in the freezer for at least 30 minutes. When you're ready to serve, take them directly from the freezer to the table.

3 cups water, divided
1 cup sugar
½ cup mint leaves, fresh, plus more, for garnish
½ cup basil leaves, fresh, washed
1 tablespoon lemon juice, freshly squeezed

In a saucepan add 1 cup water and sugar. Bring to a boil over medium-high heat. Reduce heat to low and simmer for 5 minutes, stirring constantly. Remove from stove and place in refrigerator until chilled. In a blender (or food processor) add mint, basil, juice and remaining 2 cups water and puree. Again place in refrigerator until chilled. In an ice cream maker add chilled sugar syrup and herbal water and process according to manufacturer's instructions. Transfer sorbet to a covered bowl and place in freezer until ready to serve. (Sorbet may be made ahead and kept in freezer for up to 2 months.)

To serve, scoop into martini glasses (or any other clear glass dessert dish). Place mint on top, for garnish. Serve frozen. Makes 8 servings.

Etc.

A sorbet is a frozen dessert that has a granular texture and is made with a fruit juice and syrup combination. Also known as granitas or Italian ices, they are thought to be the first iced dessert ever created. Sorbets are often confused with a sherbet (commonly mispronounced as "sherbert"), which has a creamier texture because of the fats that are added such as milk or cream.

CCKC's Ginger Mint Tea

We have served this refreshing and healthy tea at The Culinary Center for many years. It is a great alternative to sugary pop! Garnish with fresh mint sprigs and you just upped the ante on this drink's ability to aid in digestion!

1 (6-inch) piece ginger root, fresh, peeled, whole
3 to 4 cups water
4 to 6 cups green tea, brewed
Mint leaves, fresh, whole, washed, dried, for garnish

In a saucepan add ginger and water. Cook on medium-high heat for 5 to 7 minutes or until it begins to boil. Remove from heat and set aside. In a large pitcher add brewed tea. Pour in the ginger water (through a strainer to capture pieces of ginger) and stir to combine. Serve over ice with a mint leaf, for garnish, if desired. Makes 7 to 10 cups

'Fire and Ice' Mango Sorbet

Ice cream with chilies in it, you say?? Yep, we sure did...and it's good! Take a walk on the wild side, will ya?

2 cups fresh mango, fresh peeled, diced (or frozen)
½ cup water
½ pound sugar
½ cup water
½ cup corn syrup
3 to 4 serrano chilies, washed, minced

In a food processor add mango and water. Puree until combined. Set aside. In a saucepot add sugar, water and corn syrup. Place on low heat and cook until the liquid reaches a syrupy consistency. Remove from heat. Add mango purée and chilies. Stir to combine well. (Strain, if desired.) Place liquid in an ice-cream maker and freeze according to the manufacturer's instructions. Serve frozen. Makes 8 to10 servings.

Etc.

It you've never tried green tea, you're missing out on one of the world's most healthy beverages. This variety of tea was created in China and is made from tea leaves that have minimum oxidation when processed. Green tea is also very high in antioxidants, which is why it has such huge health benefits.

Fresh Fig Chutney

I always look forward to fig season – makes me feel like I'm in Italy. It's a treat to slice open a fresh fig! Create this easy fig chutney and serve it on a cheese board next to some sliced fresh fig and your favorite cheeses. Makes a great hostess gift too!

1-½ cups red wine vinegar
¾ cup light brown sugar, packed
1 onion, peeled, chopped
¼ cup ginger root, fresh, peeled, chopped
1-½ teaspoons yellow mustard seeds
Zest of ¼ lemon
½ cinnamon stick
1-¾ teaspoons salt
¼ teaspoon ground allspice
⅛ teaspoon ground cloves
1-¼ pounds figs, fresh, firm, slightly under ripe, rinsed, stems removed, sliced in half

In a large saucepan add vinegar, sugar, onion, ginger, mustard seeds, zest, cinnamon, salt, allspice, and cloves. Bring to a boil over medium-high heat, stirring occasionally. Reduce heat to low and simmer until mixture is thickened, reduced by 2/3 and forms a thick syrup consistency. Add the figs. Cook for 30 minutes or until figs are very soft and begin to fall apart and most of the liquid they have produced has evaporated. Remove from heat and transfer chutney to a non-reactive container. Set aside to come to room temperature before serving. Serve warm. Makes about 2 cups.

Etc.

This fresh fig chutney may be made up to 3 weeks in advance and stored in the refrigerator in air-tight containers. Alternately, hot chutney may be ladled into hot sterilized canning jars and processed in a hot-water bath according to manufacturer's directions.

Lemongrass Sorbet

A bright idea for a dessert or a palate cleanser between courses.

½ cup lemongrass, washed, chopped (available in Asian markets or larger grocery stores)
6 cups water
4 tablespoons lemon juice, freshly squeezed
2-¼ cups sugar
2 large egg whites

In a saucepan add lemongrass, water, juice, and sugar. Bring liquid to a boil; then reduce heat to low and simmer for 10 to 15 minutes. Remove from heat. Using a sieve (or cheesecloth), strain liquid into a bowl and set aside to cool. In a mixing bowl add egg whites. Using a hand mixer, whip until mixture forms stiff peaks. Gently whisk egg whites into sugar liquid. Transfer to an ice cream machine and freeze according to manufacturer's instructions or for 40 minutes. Transfer to an air-tight container and place in freezer until ready to serve. (Sorbet will keep in the freezer for up to 3 months.) Serve frozen. Makes approximately 6 cups.

Etc.

This sorbet has a very nice, clean subtleness to it. Serve in glass bowls for a casual family dinner or in fluted glasses for a more elegant dinner party.

Sautéed Pineapple, Cucumber and Pine Nut Relish

A fabulous little dish to serve as an appetizer with chips or as a sauce with entrées. Have some fun with this recipe while you learn what happens to cucumbers and pineapple when they are sautéed!

Spray oil, for pan
2 to 3 large cucumbers, washed, seeded, finely diced
1 pineapple, fresh, peeled, cored, finely diced
1 large red onion, finely diced
1 jalapeno pepper, washed, seeded, finely diced
½ bunch cilantro, fresh, washed, chopped
1 cup toasted pine nuts
¼ cup red wine vinegar
¾ cup olive oil
Salt and freshly ground black pepper to taste

In a sauté pan sprayed with oil add cucumbers and pineapple. Saute on medium-high heat for 3 to 5 minutes or until soft, stirring constantly to prevent scorching. Remove from heat and transfer to a mixing bowl to cool. Add onion, jalapeno, cilantro, pine nuts, vinegar, oil, salt, and pepper. Using a large spoon, mix well. Add to cucumber-pineapple mixture. Cover with plastic wrap and set aside to cool for one hour. Serve at room temperature. Makes 2 to 3 cups.

Etc.

There are many varieties of hot peppers available in grocery stores and sold at farmers markets. The red and green ones are virtually the same – the red are just left on the vine a bit longer. It's important to use the kinds that are specified in recipes so that the taste (and heat) isn't altered from the desired finished dish. "Heat index" is the term that you can look for to determine the hotness of a chili pepper. Always wash your hands with soap and water after handling a jalapeno (some folks wear plastic gloves to protect their hands) and be careful not to touch your eyes or put your fingers in your mouth – the oils are very hot and will burn.

Tomato Confiture

Confiture is a French word for a fresh jam or preserve. This one is interesting because it is made with tomatoes. Those in the know will have already arrived at the fact that a tomato is actually a fruit and not a vegetable. Go figure.

14 ounces canned tomatoes, whole, peeled, seeded
½ cup sugar
2 tablespoons water
1 cinnamon stick
¼ teaspoon ground nutmeg
⅛ teaspoon ground allspice
¼ teaspoon salt
1 tablespoon hot pepper sauce (optional)

In a small saucepan add tomatoes, sugar, water, cinnamon, nutmeg, allspice, salt, and sauce. Bring to a simmer over low heat and cook for 30 minutes, stirring occasionally. Remove from heat.

Using a slotted spoon, remove cinnamon stick and discard. Serve warm, cold or at room temperature. Refrigerate remainder for up to one week.
Makes about 1-1/2 to 2 cups.

Etc.

You may use the sauce in this recipe "as is", or puree in a blender (or food processor) for a smoother consistency. You could also use it as a stuffing for fresh strawberries by omitting the hot pepper sauce.

Recipe Index

SMALL PLATES AND STARTERS
Artichoke, Asiago and Spinach Dip, 6
Blue Cheese, Bacon and Onion Savory Cheesecake, 7
Brie en Croute with Apricot Chutney, 8
Crab Diablo Stuffed Mushrooms, 9
Curried Mango Shimp, 10
Devilishly Good Deviled Eggs, 11
Gougeres, 12
"Inside Out" Crab Rangoon Dip with Wonton Chips, 13
Sweet Potato Empanadas with Beef Picadillo
    Filling and Harissa Sauce, 14
Moroccan Market Spicy Roasted Nuts, 16
"Secret Ingredient" Spinach Dip, 17
Truffled Lentil Spoons with Bacon Vinaigrette, 18
White-Bean and Swiss Chard Bruschetta, 20

SALAD AND DRESSINGS
Asian Noodle Salad with Spicy Soy Dressing, 22
Endive and Apple Salad with Toasted Walnuts and
    Champagne Vinaigrette, 23
Fig Balsamic Vinaigrette, 24
Miso-Sesame Vinaigrette, 25
Ruthie's Spinach Salad, 26
Simple Lime-Cilantro Slaw, 27
Salad Greens with Baked Goat Cheese and
    Port-Pancetta Dressing, 28
Strawberry Balsamic Vinaigrette, 29
Tandoori Chicken Salad, 30
Tuscan Panzanella Salad, 31

SOUPS
Butternut Squash Soup, 34
Curried Carrot Soup, 35
Dublin Coddle, 36
Leek and Asparagus Soup with Boursin Cheese, 37
Lentil Soup with Moroccan Spices, 38
Low-Fat Black Bean Soup, 39
Potage Saint-Germain, 40
Spicy Corn Chowder, 41
Tomato Cognac Soup, 42
Tuscan Bean Soup, 43

MAIN DISHES
"All Hands For Hunger"™ Chicken Scallopini, 46
Almond-Crusted Cod with Roasted Sweet Potatoes, 47
Beer Braised Brisket, 48
Chicken Spiedini with Amogia Sauce, 49
Cowboy KC Strip with Tobacco Onions, 50
Grilled Lamb with Rosemary, 51
Doris Laiben's Ultimate Eggplant Parmesan Casserole, 52
Grilled Salmon with Fresh Corn and Tomato Sauté, 54
Leek & Tomato Quiche, 55
Mom's Holiday Brisket, 56
Potato-Encrusted Tilapia Filet with Two Sauces, 57
Pork Rack with Apricot Cognac Sauce, 58
Tuscan-Style Strip Steak, 60
Shrimp in Garlic Cream with Mushrooms
    and Penne Pasta, 61

PASTA
Chocolate Pasta, 64
Giacomo's Baked Pasta Dish, 65
"Grown Up" Mac 'n Cheese, 66
Lemon-Pine Nut Tagliatelle, 68
Linguini with Red Onion Marmalade, 69
Nonna's Orzo Pasta with Sun-Dried
    Tomatoes and Pesto, 70
Noodles with Thai-Vietnamese Peanut Sauce, 72
Orichiette Con Cimi di Rapa, 73
Pumpkin and Three Cheese Ravioli with
    Sage Walnut Butter Sauce, 74
Spaghetti alla Norma, 76

VEGETARIAN AND SIDE DISHES
Baked Peppers with Ricotta and Basil, 80
Barley and Wild Mushroom Risotto, 81
Crispy "Oven Fried" Red Potatoes, 82
Frijoles Charros, 83
Grilled Polenta Cakes, 84
Pan-Roasted Corn with Chilies, 85
Rice Pilaf with White Raisins, Cognac and Pistachio Nuts, 85
Simply Elegant Potato Gratin with Gruyere, 86
Wild Rice and Orzo with Toasted Walnuts and
    Dried Cranberries, 87
Wild Mushroom Cheese Tart, 88
Broccoli Soufflé, 90

BREADS
Apricot Croissant Casserole, 92
Buttermilk Cheddar Biscuits, 93
The Culinary Center's Focaccia Dough, 94
Irish Brown Bread, 95
English Digestive Biscuits
    with Blue Cheese Brandy Butter, 96
Weekend Morning Currant Scones, 98

DESSERTS
Amy- Grammer's Old-Fashioned Apple Pie, 100
Blueberry Citrus Tart, 102
Chipotle Brownies, 103
Chocolate Pepper Cookies, 104
Choco-Cappuccino Shortbread Cookies, 105
Dokey's Coconut Dream Pie, 106
Ginger Blueberry Crème Brûlée, 108
Lavender Pound Cake, 109
Luscious Berry Dessert "Soup", 110
Milk Chocolate Hazelnut Crème Brûlée, 111
Our Favorite Italian Biscotti, 112
Pumpkin Pie Cake, 113
Spanish Churros with Chocolate Dipping Sauce, 114
Strawberries in Peppered Wine Sauce, 115
Your New Favorite Cookie, 116

LITTLE EXTRAS
Aioli, 118
Asiago Alfredo Sauce, 118
Basic Marinara Sauce, 119
Basil Mint Sorbet, 120
Ginger Mint Tea, 121
'Fire and Ice' Mango Sorbet, 121
Fresh Fig Chutney, 122
Lemongrass Sorbet, 123
Sautéed Pineapple, Cucumber and Pine Nut Relish, 124
Tomato Confiture, 125

About the Author

Laura Laiben

Laura grew up in a small German community in Missouri where her passion for the culinary arts began at a young age with making pastry dough with her Grandmother while sitting on her kitchen counter. Laura practiced corporate, securities and public finance law for 18 years before jumping career tracks to design and open The Culinary Center of Kansas City. She believes strongly in the concept of social entrepreneurship, commitment to community and the philosophy that "if you do good, you'll do good."

She has extensive teaching, teambuilding facilitating and special event planning experience as well as a rich background in the practice of business and finance. This is her second cookbook following "Best Recipes – First Collection" published in 2000. Ms. Laiben and The Culinary Center are featured regularly in many local publications, TV and radio and she has also been featured on the cover of "Family Money," a nationally distributed magazine. She is a featured speaker on the topics of small business, social entrepreneurship, risk, business and personal mentoring, career changes and the practice of following your heart when it comes to your career. She was honored in 2003 as one of the "Top 25 Women Who Mean Business in Kansas City" by the Kansas City Small Business Monthly, has been an active member of the Helzberg Entrepreneurial Mentoring Program since 2003 and was honored as one of the "Most Influential Women In Kansas City" in 2011. The Culinary Center of Kansas City has been awarded many honors: 2008 Impact Award, 1999 President's Award by The Downtown Overland Park Partnership for its contribution to the business and community in Overland Park, Kansas and the ACF's 2007 Greater Kansas City Chefs Association's prestigious Presidents Award. However her favorite award to date is the "Best Places To Work" in Kansas City awarded in 2012. Laura is living her dream. Go figure!